QUILT
OUT
LOUD

Activism, Language &
the Art of Quilting

THOMAS KNAUER

ONE IN SIX
WILL BE
ATTEM

stashBOOKS®
an imprint of C&T Publishing

Text and artwork copyright © 2023 by Thomas Knauer

Photography © 2023 by C&T Publishing, Inc.

Publisher: Amy Barrett-Daffin

Creative Director: Gailen Runge

Senior Editor: Roxane Cerda

Technical Editor: Kathryn Patterson

Cover/Book Designer: April Mostek

Production Coordinator: Tim Manibusan

Illustrator: Mary Flynn and Thomas Knauer

Photography Coordinator: Lauren Herberg

Photography Assistant: Rachel Ackley

Screenshots by Thomas Knauer

Front cover photography by Lauren Herberg

Photography by Lauren Herberg of C&T Publishing, Inc., unless otherwise noted

Published by Stash Books, an imprint of C&T Publishing, Inc., P.O. Box 1456, Lafayette, CA 94549

Library of Congress Cataloging-in-Publication Data

Names: Knauer, Thomas, author.

Title: Quilt out loud : activism, language & the art of quilting / Thomas Knauer.

Description: Lafayette, CA : Stash Books, [2023] | Summary: "Quilters will learn how the use of letters, numbers, words, and sentences change when used on quilts rather than a screen or paper. Quilt Out Loud features a wide variety of techniques for making text a part of quilts and two projects on embedding messages in quilts"-- Provided by publisher.

Identifiers: LCCN 2022032956 | ISBN 9781644033227 (trade paperback) | ISBN 9781644033234 (ebook)

Subjects: LCSH: Patchwork--Patterns. | Quilting--Patterns. | Lettering. | Textile crafts--Social aspects.

Classification: LCC TT835 .K56365 2023 | DDC 746.46/041--dc23/eng/20220808

LC record available at https://lccn.loc.gov/2022032956

Printed in China

10 9 8 7 6 5 4 3 2 1

Epigraph /

I know of no genius but the genius of hard work.
~J.M.W. Turner

Dedication

For Dee Pop, Sylvain Sylvain & Florian Schneider. You were extraordinary.

Acknowledgments

There are so many people who aided directly or indirectly with this book that I am afraid I shan't be able to acknowledge them all. First my parents for not trying too hard to dissuade me from the life of an artist. And especially my mother who had a hand in binding most of these quilts; yay you! Of course, all the professors over the years who believed in the art student who never made anything. And obviously my family, my brilliant wife, and extraordinary children; you all make everything worthwhile.

Now, practically speaking I'd like to thank my editor Roxane Cerda for taking a leap on this book and then doing so much to shape it into a respectable form. And my agent Kate McKean for her advocacy, advice, and all-around awesomeness. And Lisa Sipes, who was the first quilter I worked with; you taught me what might be able to be done and greatly expanded my universe. And Shelly Pagliai for taking on a beast of a project and delivering masterfully. And then Jennifer Strauser for taking on the majority of my recent quilts in great big stacks without blinking an eye and making magic. Oh, and I can't forget Handi Quilter for sharing its machine with me for so many years, allowing me to do things no one else would.

Then there is April Mostek for making the book so beautiful. And Amy Barrett-Daffin for greenlighting this one; I am glad to have found such a good home for this book. And, of course, everyone in creative who had their fingers on this book, or at least the keyboards that were used to put this book together. You all have my undying appreciation for working so hard on my little project.

Finally, I'd like to thank coffee, punk rock, and whisky for helping me write all the words. Without you, I'd still probably be staring at a blank Word document.

CONTENTS

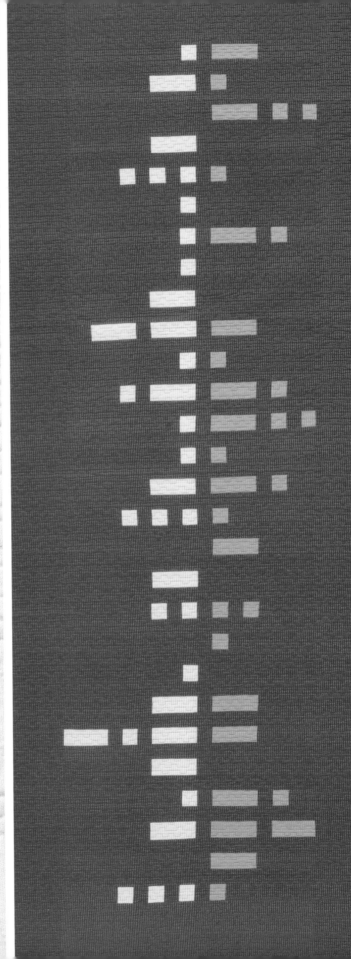

FORE
WORD

AS ARTISTS, we are taught to expect that our audiences will only passively engage with our work. The expectation, by and large, is that they will be immersed in it briefly, which will elicit superficial praise. Those who view it may even use phrases such as "beautiful" or "amazing" when referencing our work. They may tell a friend or two about their experience. However, the engagement stops there. We come to appreciate that audiences want to see our work at all, and we set aside the questions about and critiques of society that drove us to create the art in the first place. With the growing prominence of social justice art, in all its forms, and the rise of several civil rights movements backed by social media, we have realized that we want the art we create to encourage action. We want our work to cause audiences to challenge their beliefs, confront their biases, learn different perspectives, and move toward being an ally or co-conspirator. *Quilt Out Loud* provides the technical foundation and artistic inspiration for us to do so.

Art is meant to speak to your soul. It holds space for education, reflection, healing, and curiosity. Art is an indirect and ongoing dialogue. It involves an unspoken language that bridges communities and perspectives. It gives a voice to those perpetually silenced. Art at its foundation is a form of resistance. Thomas Knauer highlights artists and visionaries who utilize art and, more specifically, quilting, to embark on a journey of brave and bold activism. These artists have mastered the juxtaposition of the delicateness of thread and fabric with the evocative nature of the statements each of their quilts holds. Their work asks us to rethink the relationship between the textile world, historically seen as a private and elite sphere, and contemporary society, which is struggling under the weight of the current socio-political climate.

The question of whether quilting is an appropriate platform to convey social justice issues may come to mind. Quilting is a peaceful hobby that is often associated with comfort, warmth, protection, and in some cases, decoration. But, quilting also has a long history as a form of activism. Since the 19th century, quilts have been used as a means of addressing social issues, from women's suffrage and child labor exploitation, to inequality and racial discrimination. *The Queen's Quilt*, by Queen Lili'uokalani' from 1895 and Faith Ringgold's, *Story Quilts* of the 1960s are early examples. Their quilts utilized imagery and symbolism as well as embroidered, pieced, and painted text to convey their anti-colonial, anti-racist, and feminist messages. In *Quilt Out Loud* Thomas Knauer encourages us to take the quilts we create a step further by including text. He illuminates the relationship between language and art: how one influences the other and the possibility for the conflation of the two. He reminds us of the power of language and the familiarity of textiles. He utilizes our prior relationships with quilts to get our feet in the door, while the messaging on the quilts keeps us firmly planted. We are left both in awe of the art and captivated by the striking use of language. Each piece included in *Quilt Out Loud* is an invitation. An invitation into the world of the artist. An invitation to hear their voice and their story. However, it is also an invitation to act. An invitation to mobilize and advocate. An invitation to utilize the techniques outlined to develop our own social justice quilts.

At the Social Justice Sewing Academy (SJSA), we aim to empower individuals to become art activists and to utilize textile art as a medium to amplify social justice issues. Through the creation of blocks, mini quilts, and community quilts, individuals are encouraged to engage in truth-telling through cloth. The experiences of each individual are woven into every stitch and augmented by color, use of language, improvisation, and abstraction. The art created reflects each individual's understanding of the world around them. We call into question all preconceived notions about what quilting is, what it should be, and who should engage in it. Similarly, the quilts in *Quilt Out Loud* provide a mirror in which we can see ourselves reflected in the artist's experiences. We understand how the artist's cultural relationships with cotton fabrics influenced the quilts that they produced. We see that quilts became a means of processing emotions regarding the many ills of society. We resonate with the need to be heard in a world that frequently invalidates and ignores certain experiences. *Quilt Out Loud* provides a window from which we can see ourselves creating art that is rooted in much of the same purpose.

~ **Sara Trail,** FOUNDER OF THE
SOCIAL JUSTICE SEWING ACADEMY

INTRO

Why Words?

I think about words a lot. I mean *a lot*. Not so much individual words and what they mean, but how words work, the fact that they work at all. There is nothing natural about the words we use; they only work, have meaning, through our unconscious collective agreement that they do, in fact, work. I have always found something beautiful about the fact that beneath all of our conversations and arguments we have to share a common tongue.

And beyond that basic agreement on the meaning of words, I am deeply interested in the different forms that words can take. The spoken word works very differently than the written word; the first requires a certain proximity, and even intimacy, while the latter can be received at times and places remote from its origin. The difference between the handwritten, the printed, and the digital could take me down a rabbit hole, so suffice it to say I am enamored with the complexity of the words we so often take for granted.

Now, to the matter at hand. Why words on quilts? Well, I think of quilts as generational objects, memory holders that are passed from one to another over the years. If quilts were books, they would be leather-bound volumes made to survive the vicissitudes of use. In adding language to quilts, we write messages that are intended for those to come.

DUCTION

They may speak to us in the present, but like all quilts they resonate with history as the decades pass. What I write (or piece or appliqué) now will be experienced for years to come.

But what I think makes text quilts truly unique is that they are written documents that are intended for use in someone's life. The message is slept with, encountered first thing in the morning and last thing at night. Text quilts work in distinctly different ways than, say, posters or paintings. Quilts are not just to be looked at; they are lived with, and therefore so is the text that quilts carry with them.

So why words? Text quilts offer us another way to speak, to use our voices to reaffirm ourselves, to protest a wrong, to lay bare our emotions. In *Quilt Out Loud* we will be exploring myriad techniques for creating text quilts as well as the conceptual implications of different types of language. While we make these quilts we explicitly will be making meaning and perhaps even making sense of the world around us.

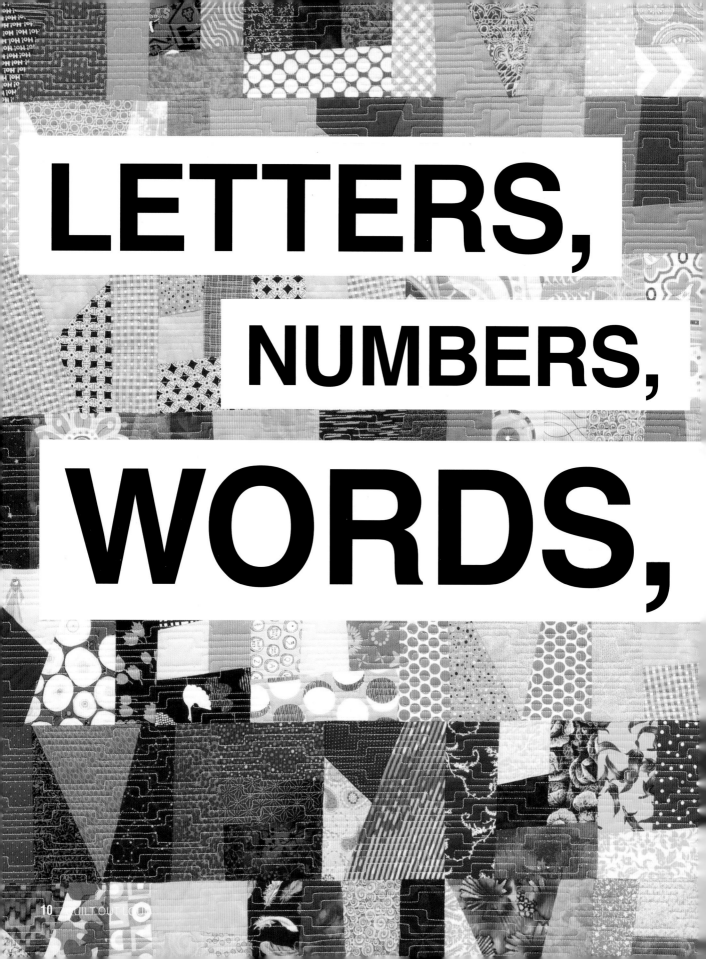

LETTERS, NUMBERS, WORDS,

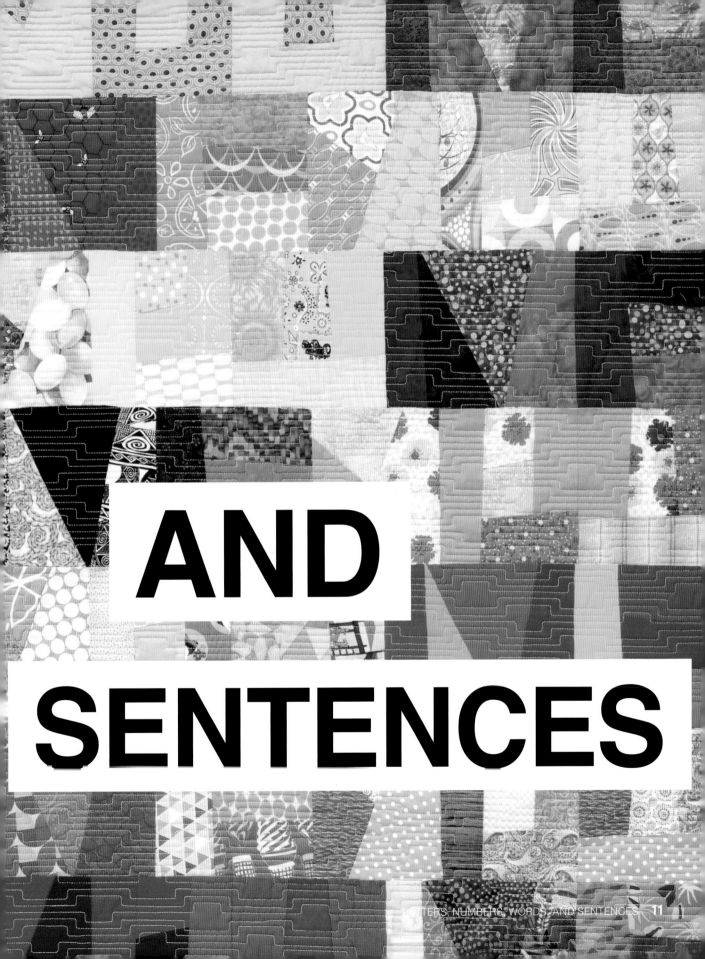

AND
SENTENCES

LANGUAGE
is a remarkable thing.

When spoken, it is ephemeral; our words are quite literally air. When written down, language takes on a solidity and becomes substance. In written language, letters and words are made of … stuff. Of something. Whether it be electronic signal, ink on paper, or even cloth, all letters are made, fundamentally, of raw materials. It is this reality that makes material language so remarkable. While the spoken word lasts for a specific period of time and then disappears, or is replaced by new words, material language allows us to engage it for however long we like. When reading, we can linger over a single word or speed across the page. The reader, the recipient, decides just how much time to spend with a text.

While there are certain commonalities between all material texts, I believe that quilts hold unique possibilities for displaying material information and for sharing ideas and emotions. There is nothing unique about cloth per se, but when it is transformed into a quilt, it enters into a robust vocabulary of meaning. Because quilts already have so much meaning attached to them, the text that a given quilt may carry is imbued with that history alongside the unique meaning conveyed by the letters, numbers, words, or sentences that it bears.

Furthermore, every kind of text has its own specific duration: A poster is meant to hold you for a moment, a book for the length of a book (or longer, if it merits rereading). For the most part, a material text offers only a passing relationship, one distinct from the spoken word, but one that is measured in seconds and minutes, days and weeks. Quilts, on the other hand, are generational objects, meant to be passed down in families and among friends and loved ones. Regardless of the initial recipient, the time frame of a quilt is measured in decades, and if lucky, centuries. This lengthy time span of quilts brings with it a particular understanding of text on quilts.

So quilts. The first thing we need to recognize about quilts is that they carry the marks of the labor that went into their making: the patchwork and quilting that manifest directly on their surfaces.

While we know that various forms of labor go into every material text, the method of their making is rarely so directly observable; it may take years to write a novel, but in the book we have only the end result, not the process. A quilt, on the other hand, carries its maker with it. Hence, the text on a quilt is both removed from the spoken word and imbued with it via the eternal presence of its making.

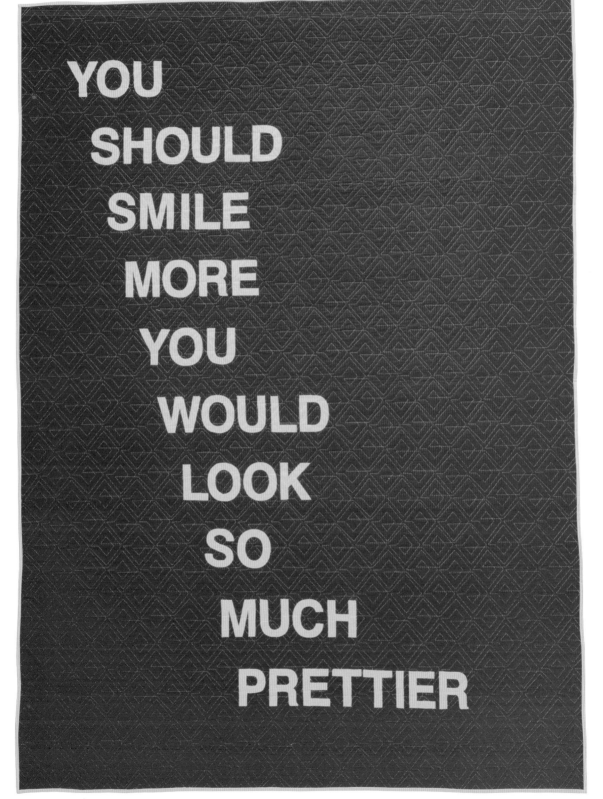

Advice from an Eighth Grade PE Teacher, 60″ × 80″, 2022, designed and pieced by Thomas Knauer, quilted by Jennifer Strauser

Next we move on to the
TEMPORALITY of quilts.

Every quilt occupies a double time frame: the immediate experience and the understanding of its past and future use. In our house we fall asleep with quilts and then wake with them as well; these quilts usher us into our dreams and provide reminders as we start our days. But while there is an immediacy to the engagement with a quilt, underneath there is always an awareness of the generational nature of the quilt. We often sleep with quilts made by my wife's grandmother, thereby creating a connection not only to her but to the time of the quilt's making. In these quilts the past is perpetually present. My quilts, on the other hand, exist with the presumption of a long future, of uses to come by people who do not yet exist. A quilt always carries this other time along with it: a past or a future that saturates the material of the quilt in the now.

In this context, a quilt with text is a unique and entangled manner of writing: The letters and numbers, words and sentences, entwine with the other fundamental aspects of being with a quilt. The text has an immediate impact, and we react to it through the lens of our own experience and against the backdrop of our current social, cultural, and political climates. At the same time, when we read text on a quilt, we imagine how it might have been received in the past or how it might be understood in the future. It speaks as an enduring statement, one that will be passed down with the quilt across years and decades. Thus, the reading of text on a quilt pulls us in two directions, toward a short and a long time span. Even as we find meaning in the words, we simultaneously wonder whether those words may still be relevant in years to come.

In Defense of Handmade, 90˝ × 90˝, 2014, designed and pieced by Thomas Knauer, quilted by Lisa Sipes
International Quilt Museum, University of Nebraska–Lincoln, 2016.063.0001, www.internationalquiltmuseum.org

Finally, we must understand a quilt with words as a text that is lived with day to day, year after year.

In this way the text remakes itself anew with every change we experience. For example, a COVID quilt will pass (I hope) from a writing born of immediacy to one that speaks from the realm of memory. As long as the quilt is being used, the words it carries will fit themselves into our lives. Because that text is part of our daily lives and is altered (worn) by its use, it is never a static text; it resists the stagnation of a book sitting unread on a shelf.

Beyond considering the basic presence of text on a quilt, we need to explore the meaning of different methods of applying text. Various forms of appliqué, piecing, and coded text speak in distinctly different ways: While the words are not necessarily different, each technique carries its own unique tonality. Later in the book I will explore the various how-tos of text quilts, but for now let's explore the conceptual implications of several of these processes.

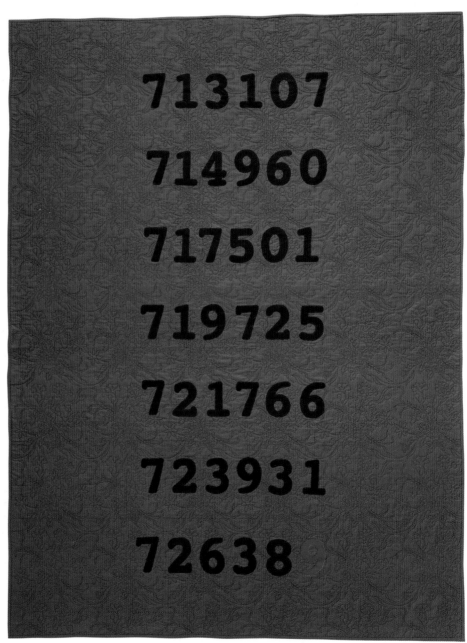

COVID: 11–17 October 2021, 60″ × 80″, 2022, designed and pieced by
Thomas Knauer, quilted by Jennifer Strauser

With appliqué we stitch material—in the cases discussed in this book, letters and numbers—onto the surface of the quilt top. When finished, the appliqué sits on top of the background fabric. In this way, appliqué is quite similar to some of the other fine arts, painting in particular: The layering of fabric in appliqué is like the application of layers of paint. This layering is fundamental to appliqué; the appliquéd fabric will jump to the fore, like the writing on a page. While the background recedes materially, it is nonetheless important; it lays out a space for the appliqué to play upon, to respond to. Rather than being a blank slate, the background is another essential layer in the quilt.

ME/YOU/US, 58½˝ × 58½˝, 2016, from the Handi Quilter Corporate Collection

Reverse appliqué, on the other hand, is just the opposite. Our letters are cut through and removed from the uppermost surface of the quilt top. Here the process more closely resembles carving; it is an intrusive incising of material. But unlike carving, which aims to produce a solid form, reverse appliqué opens up a window in the surface of the quilt top to allow another material to show through. In this case we are drawn into the secondary layer of the quilt top, pulled past the immediate encounter to something revealed below.

The practice of piecing letters, of creating letterforms out of carefully constructed patchwork, is an entirely different process. Here the letters and numbers reside on the same layer as the rest of the quilt top and are therefore conceptually entwined with the totality of the quilt top. With pieced letters there is no substrate, just surface. Like all patchwork, it is a fractured surface but a single surface nonetheless. Here patchwork and language may comingle, play one off of the other to create quilt tops of bold simplicity or exquisite complexity.

In piecing our text we assert an equality of language and design, one inextricable from the other.

Beyond choosing a method for handling the cloth, we have the question of the language itself. While it may seem self-evident to add text in one's native language, we could consider using various encoded languages, languages that are formed by things other than traditional letters. We might use Morse code and piece in dots and dashes, use Braille and let the letter-units that make up the language guide our piecing decisions, or even use binary code and play with any number of ways to visualize the *0*s and *1*s that tell computers which letters to display. And there is something quite wonderful about encoding a message, hiding it from the ordinary viewer so that it may be shared only with those we let in on its meaning. While quilts with alphanumeric lettering proclaim themselves, encoded quilts are secrets seldom shared.

Troth (Pride), 80˝ × 80˝, 2015

Thus far we have been considering only fabric as our textual material, but we have a second vocabulary for speaking through our quilts: the quilting itself. Here we have what can be an entirely independent voice written on and over the piecing but not following it. Quilted text is almost ephemeral; it lacks the solidity of cloth. Even so, it is resolutely there. So many possibilities open up when quilting with text: It may reinforce the idea of the quilt or contradict it and produce a meaningful tension. We could even go all the way to wholecloth and allow the quilting to be the singular voice. In quilting with text we are writing in the quilt, through it even, stitching together all three layers. I always find it a beautiful visual—and material—metaphor to have letters and numbers, words and sentences, holding my quilt together.

Your Heritage Is Written in Other People's Blood, 74″ × 74″, 2018

BEYOND THESE TECHNIQUES
there remains a wide array of alternative approaches for getting text into or onto a quilt.

For example, on-demand fabric printing platforms are excellent for simply printing your text onto cloth, whether it be individual letters, words, or entire texts. In this space we are not confined by the limits of our materials but can do almost anything we can imagine. And of course, embroidery is a traditional and powerful way of applying text to a quilt. There is a certain intimacy about embroidered text in the frequently vast space of a quilt that renders it delicate, precious even. Finally, there are all manners of pigments made for use on fabric, thus allowing us to simply write or paint our text directly onto the quilt top. This perhaps offers a profound sense of urgency quite distinct from the precision needed for appliqué and piecing.

So armed with a battery of ideas about and approaches to making textual quilts, the only thing we need now is something to say: our own letters and numbers, words and sentences. In the end, that is what it's really all about: not just putting some words on a quilt but finding and using our voices. I make text quilts to get out and put down whatever is roiling in my mind; to express my ideas and emotions; to speak about today, and along with that, the past and the future. There is so much unsaid that ought to find voice, and there are words too important to scribble on a piece of paper inevitably to be lost in the shuffle. I like to think of these quilts as a means of writing that which we should never forget.

Yes, text on quilts can be weighty and can carry enormous significance, but it also can be a means for play, a means of bringing delight. A few precious words to a loved one or a poem for a friend can be joys that we carry with us from place to place and across the span of time. What we write ranges from the tragic to the joyful, from obscure to precise, from angry to loving. Indeed, there is no wrong direction for the letters, numbers, words, and sentences we may choose as long as we are using our voices to say what needs to be said.

On Generating Text

The trickiest part of working with text may well be determining just which text to use. Should it be something original or a quotation? Long or short? Metaphoric or literal? Because our lives proliferate with text, there is perpetually so much to choose from. And unlike abstract shapes, text will always carry meaning, meaning that must be reconciled with its presence on a quilt made of cloth and thread (which is a unique and evocative textual placement).

Personally, I am a fan of quotations—borrowed text—because such texts always reach out beyond the scope of the quilt.

Borrowed texts can be found via simple internet searches, and they become connected to other, similar texts. My *Funerary Quilts*, for example, borrow text from newspaper reports about police shootings of unarmed African American men. Each quoted text connects to the fuller story as reported, which in turn connects the tragic reality of the killing of unarmed African Americans. Thus, with quoted text you are simultaneously working with other adjacent texts, which, when brought back to the context of the text on your quilt, inevitably makes a much larger statement.

On the other hand, an original text brings with it a certain intimacy, the sharing of an inner voice. In externalizing text that heretofore had been private, you are inviting the viewer of the quilt into your space, opening up the possibility for a personal connection. While borrowed text embeds itself in a larger sphere of texts, an original text functions more as an invitation, a moment of communal engagement between maker and viewer. The original text is a gesture of opening up, of being vulnerable through the quilt. Where a borrowed text is inevitably a statement about the world, an original text declares the presence of an individual self, a being in the world, a voice.

This is not to say that a borrowed text cannot be intimate, or that original text does not make a statement about the wider world. Each mode of text inherently does so many things by existing on a quilt and asks a good deal of the viewer in interpreting the meaning that it is hard to go astray. But I do have one final bit of advice: Do everything you can to avoid cliché because clichéd texts inevitably ring inauthentic through their overuse, and the great power of text on quilts is that it offers the chance to connect intellectually, emotionally, and aesthetically with viewers, which is a remarkable power indeed.

Denyse Schmidt

I made my first quilt with words back in 1999 or so. A few years before that, I was studying graphic design. I was into hand lettering and carving letters in stone—any kind of lettering that wasn't precise and perfect—mainly as an antidote to the rigid influence of the department that at the time revered the Swiss approach to graphic design. I even sold a typeface based on my cut-paper letters to one of the digital foundries that were popping up at the time. Barbara Kruger's work was everywhere then, and I know that was an influence as well.

Years later, when I began making quilts, it seemed logical to do something typographic. I loved the idea that women had a history of making quilts with political (and other) messages long before they could vote—that seemed so radical and strange.

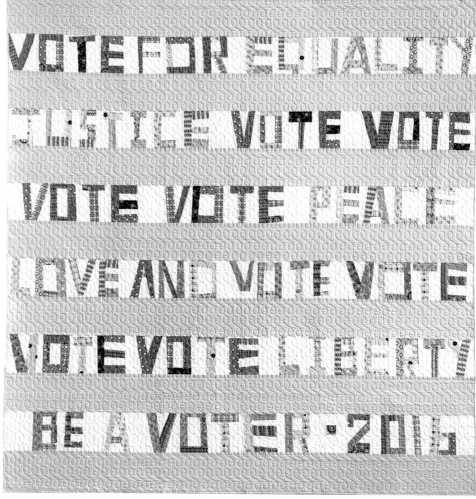

VOTE QUILT, 68˝ × 70˝, 2016, designed by Denyse Schmidt, pieced by Denyse Schmidt, quilted by Janice Roy

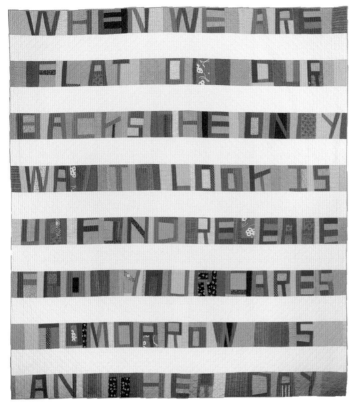

PROVERBIAL QUILT, 68″ × 88″, designed and pieced by Denyse Schmidt, hand quilted by Julie Tebay, 1992, or machine quilted by Janice Roy, 2009

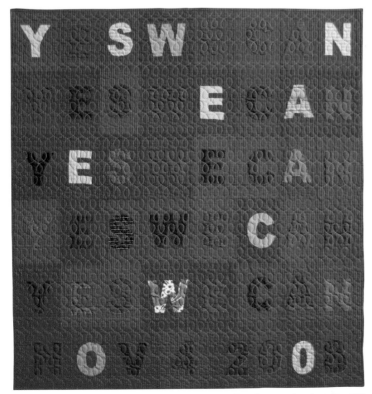

YES WE CAN, 50″ × 52″, 2008, designed by Denyse Schmidt, pieced and appliquéd by Denyse Schmidt with help from Heather Ross, quilted by Janice Roy

What to say is always the challenge (like when carving words in stone), so I decided to use an amalgamation of proverbs and fortunes from cookies. I chose phrases that related to what we do in bed—sleeping, recovering from illness bodily or otherwise, dreaming, escaping. "When we are flat on our backs, the only way to look is up. Find release from your cares, tomorrow is another day."

Many years later (2009), I made a commercial pattern for this quilt, which included the full alphabet so people could "customize, personalize, memorialize, or editorialize. You can even (if you must) dispense advice. And they can sleep on it."

The *YES WE CAN* quilt happened during the heady days leading up to the 2008 election. I have always loved Jessie Bell Williams Telfair's *Freedom* quilt (made in the 1970s or 1980s), and the red/blue palette and simple, graphic repetition of her quilt was a direct influence. I hand appliquéd the letters onto blocks while traveling. I later got it on the Obama fundraising site and managed to sell thousands of tickets to raise more than $15,000 for the campaign.

ON
APPLIQUÉ

7 33003 52

HANDMADE

26 . 1

E IN FIVE CHIL
THE UNITED S
ES HUNGRY AT
NT DURING TH

RAW-EDGE APPLIQUÉ is, hands down, the most materially immediate way to get text onto a quilt (other than a permanent marker, of course).

While the cutting out of letters may be tedious and the stitching of the appliqué on minute letters may be highly technical, it still feels more direct than any of the other methods. It is much like collage, positioning elements in just the right place in relation to each other and to the whole. With appliqué, the typographic design possibilities are nearly endless.

I have tried needle-turn appliqué for letters, but after attempting my first uppercase *E*, I gave it up as utterly futile. With the abundance of angles in so many of the characters, lettering is simply not well suited for needle-turn. But we still want clean, precise edges to our letters, and that requires a good deal of technical skill.

If you have a bit of design proficiency and the right software (I use Adobe Illustrator, so I'll be demonstrating in that environment), you can create your own reversed letters in addition to using the reversed alphabets I made for you to download. To make your own, you start with the letters or words you intend to use. I like to immediately convert my text to outlines; this makes the letters vector artwork rather than typographic information. You then select your vector letters and use the OBJECT down menu, the TRANSFORM option and the REFLECT suboption. Within the REFLECT panel, select the VERTICAL axis. And voilà, you have reversed your letters. From there you can UNGROUP your letters and reposition them however you wish.

Start with the letters or words you intend to use.

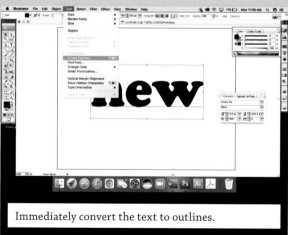

Immediately convert the text to outlines.

Select your vector letters and use the OBJECT dropdown menu, the TRANSFORM option, and the REFLECT suboption.

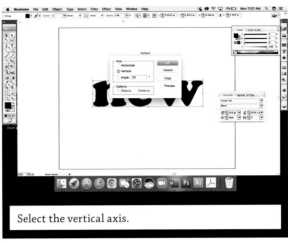

Select the vertical axis.

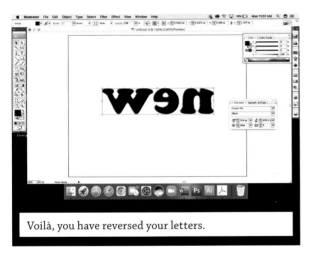

Voilà, you have reversed your letters.

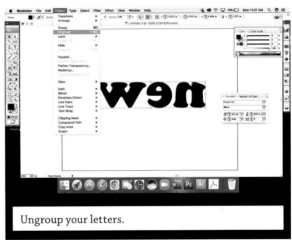

Ungroup your letters.

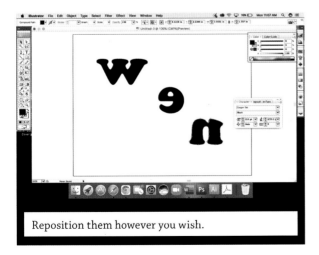

Reposition them however you wish.

First of all, I always use a paper-backed fusible (like Wonder-Under) when doing my lettering.

I trace the reversed letters onto the fusible's paper backing; the letters must be reversed for the fabric side to come out correctly oriented. I then fuse the glue side of my fusible to the wrong side of the fabric, leaving the tracing visible on the bottom side of the cloth. Now with this paper stabilizing the cloth, it is far easier to cut out letters of all sizes and maintain wonderfully clean lines. Next, I peel the paper backing away from the cloth and fuse my letter—glue side down—to my background cloth. And then comes the tricky part.

While much of the labor of quilting is done by zipping through countless quarter-inch seams, with raw-edge appliqué, we must perform a precise series of curves and turns to get around each letter. In doing my appliqué, I use a straight stitch as close to $\frac{1}{16}^{th}$ of an inch from the edge of the letter as I can get, carefully rounding the curves and repositioning as frequently as seems prudent. While it may seem infuriating to go three stitches at a time for smaller letters, the resulting crispness of effect is entirely worth it. Of course, zigzag stitching the letter edges is always an option, but I find it to be bulky, especially in tight angles. It seems to draw attention to itself in place of the cloth of the letters.

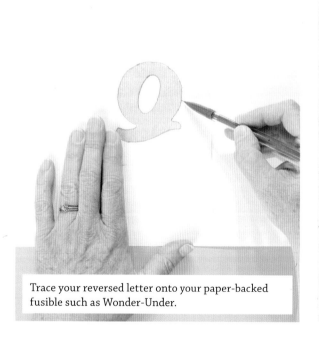

Trace your reversed letter onto your paper-backed fusible such as Wonder-Under.

Iron your fusible with the letter to the wrong side of your fabric.

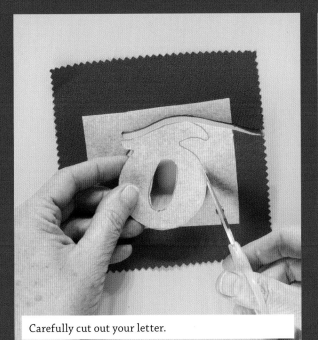

Carefully cut out your letter.

Remove the paper backing from your fusible.

Iron your letter onto your background fabric.

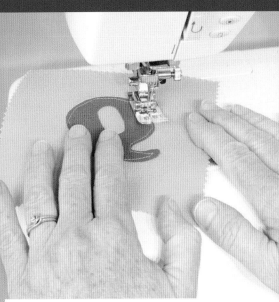

Carefully stitch your letter to your background fabric.

For me, stitching my letters and numbers to the surface of the background cloth creates a certain solidity for each character, a presence that is resolutely *on* the quilt. I tend to use raw-edge appliqué for most of my text quilts because it enables a very precise line: The edge of the cloth sits precisely on the backing fabric. I want my letters, just like my words, to stand out and assert themselves. Here the process of setting the type in place is much like the materiality of setting lead type, carefully positioning each letter exactly where it needs to go horizontally and vertically. It is a process that frequently involves multiple rulers' running horizontally and vertically, along with an abundance of patience, to line up everything properly.

Laying out type on a quilt can be quite a problem in and of itself before we even get to the fusing and the appliqué. Choice of the layout, the scale, and the color/pattern all flavor the intonation of the text, the way it might be spoken aloud. Small text is a whisper; large text, perhaps, is a shout. The first step in any typographic quilt is to decide which kind of voice you want to use.

From there we still have the problem of good layout. I use center-justified text a lot for quilts (equal amounts of text on each side of an imaginary middle line running down the quilt). I do this because it seems to work well in relation to traditional quilts. It also feels the most direct to me: right there, no complicated layout to distract from the words themselves. This is also the approach I use for my quieter quilts, the ones I want you to get close to in order to read the text.

When working with larger text, pretty much everything is fair game: diagonals, sideways, even circular. The key to any of these approaches is to mark your quilt carefully with the starting point of each line: Measure horizontally from the right or left edge (I recommend keeping that consistent across the quilt to keep things easy and organized), and measure vertically from the top or bottom to find the starting point for your line of text. From that point, extend a straight line in whichever direction your text will run, giving you a baseline for that line of text. Repeat this for all your text before you begin the layout process; you will want these layout guides as you progress.

Finally, I do my layout of my cutout letters with the paper backing of the fusible still on. This makes it easy to place all my letters or numbers in the proper positions. Then I peel the paper backing off the first letter and fuse it into place; only then do I move on to the next letter. I have accidentally fused a bit of a neighboring letter too many times to remove the backing from all my letters at once. When all your letters are fused in place, then begins the actual appliqué.

While appliqué can indeed be labor intensive, it nonetheless feels like the most immediate of the traditional methods for getting text onto a quilt. When we, the makers, perform the laborious process of doing good appliqué, the viewer sees something far simpler: letters sewn to a piece of cloth. For them, the process can disappear.

Accessing the Alphabet Templates

As not everyone has the ready ability to produce reversed letters, I have prepared reversed alphabets in three fonts, each in three sizes. Select the alphabet and size you want and print just the pages you need.

To access the reversed alphabet templates, ready for appliqué and reverse appliqué, type the web address below into your browser window. tinyurl.com/11530-pattern1-download

Cooper Black

ABCDEF
GHIJKL
MNOPQR
STUVWX
YZ0123
456789

A B C D E F

G H I J K L

M N O P Q R

S T U V W X

Y Z 0 1 2 3

4 5 6 7 8 9

PT Mono Bold

A B C D E F
G H I J K L
M N O P Q R
S T U V W X
Y Z 0 1 2 3
4 5 6 7 8 9

Second Degree Rape

To my mind, the very idea of a criminal charge of second-degree rape is patently absurd; if you rape someone—no matter the circumstances—you have raped them. Period. This quilt uses a floral sheet as a background to locate the message, to give it context, and to offer the viewer a lovely—perhaps saccharine—overall field. Then by using appliqué to add the phrase Two to Seven Years (the sentencing guidelines for second-degree rape) the quilt shifts in an uncertain direction. When the title is read, the quilt finally comes together, compressing the seeming innocence of a bed sheet with the absurdly inadequate sentencing; evoking, it is hoped, some form of outrage at the idea of justifying rape in any form.

Second Degree Rape, 60″ × 80″, 2021, designed and pieced by Thomas Knauer, quilted by Jennifer Strauser

[TWO TO SEVEN YEARS]

In Defense of Handmade

This quilt uses the barcode and UPC number of a mass-produced Martha Stewart quilt as the basis for a homemade quilt. As such, this quilt explicitly critiques the devaluing of labor and individuality in modern mass production. So much of what we buy and own is made in horrible working conditions for very little pay, a model that has changed little since the beginnings of the industrial revolution. Working on handmade/homemade things is inherently a repudiation of this model of production; slow, conscientious, loving labor replaces speed and demand. This quilt was painstakingly pieced, appliquéd, and quilted as a demonstration of what the intimacy of individual labor can achieve; it is an explicit rejection of the fast, cheap, and easy economy of the twenty-first century.

In Defense of Handmade, 90″ × 90″, 2014, designed and pieced by Thomas Knauer, quilted by Lisa Sipes
International Quilt Museum, University of Nebraska–Lincoln, 2016.063.0001, www.internationalquiltmuseum.org

American Story #3

Finally, there is plain speech: simple, direct language that cuts straight to the core of the issue at hand. In this case I used a straightforward statistic to highlight the reality of childhood poverty. This is not the kind of language one expects to find on a quilt, an object that connotes safety, warmth, and even love. Against the conceptual background of a quilt, the blunt language of *American Story #3: Hunger* can act like a punch to the stomach; it becomes visceral rather than only intellectual.

A statistic lays out the measurable reality of a problem; it is inarguable, assuming the statistician is working with good data. Statistical information and other direct uses of language can require the viewer/reader to confront difficult information. The text needs to be taken in, processed, and understood. This takes time, and that time opens up a space for an emotional response. It is ultimately that emotional response that I am looking for; I am aiming to evoke empathy through the juxtaposition of harsh quantifiable truths against the comforting associations of quilts in order to craft as strong a statement as possible.

American Story #3: Hunger, 80″ × 80″, 2020,
designed and pieced by Thomas Knauer, quilted by Jennifer Strauser

Advice from an Eighth Grade PE Teacher

In my daughter's eighth-grade year, her PE teacher noticed the students were having a rough day, so the teacher advised them, "You should smile more. You would look so much prettier." Though I think he meant it kindly, he obviously did not know the history of telling women to smile. It may seem like a simple phrase, but it implicitly tells women how they should appear, how they should feel, how they should be. It reinforces a certain expectation of beauty and inevitably implies control over women's bodies. This quilt is my response for my daughter; it mirrors the original phrase through the lens of colors that produce a harsh visual effect. My hope for this quilt is that no one will be able to read the text without seeing the abrasive nature of the language that it depicts.

Advice from an Eighth Grade PE Teacher, 60″ × 80″, 2022, designed and pieced by Thomas Knauer, quilted by Jennifer Strauser

YOU
SHOULD
SMILE
MORE
YOU
WOULD
LOOK
SO
MUCH
PRETTIER

SMILE
MORE

Hillary Goodwin

Nude Is Not a Color, by Hillary Goodwin, Bianca Springer, Rachael Dorr, and several quilters throughout the world
From the Collections of the Henry Ford

People don't expect their comfort objects to portray a hard message about such things as gun violence, drug addiction, and white supremacy. Therein lies the magic of text in quilts. These messages are sewn into tokens of daily life, difficult to hide from, undeniable in their meaning, disrupting many of the stories we tell ourselves in private. The comfort and the harsh realities of life dancing together, in my opinion, is a powerful mix.

The text of the *Nude Is Not a Color* quilt came long before the idea of dressing our everywoman in a dress made of pieced dress shirts in all shades of "nude." In response to a designer who came out with a season's worth of clothing designated as the color "nude" (a light pink that does not represent the nude most women of the world understand), we made a quilt that demonstrates the diversity of skin colors among us. Our woman in the quilt shows our collective strength, and our text in the quilt tells her story.

"Nude Is Not A Color"

Contributors:

Hillary Goodwin
Rachael Darr
Nicole Neblett
Tamara King
Berene Campbell
Carmen Alonso
Anne Eriksson
Silvana Coutinho
Sandra Johnson
Rachel Singh
Alexandra Ledgerwood
Robin King
Lynn Carson Harris

Bianca Springer
Chawne Kimber
Agnes Ang
Krishma Patel
Sonia Sanchez
Maite Macias
Amy Vaughn Ready
Jess Ziegler
Michele Spirko
Rebeca Green
Kirsty Cleverly
Krista Hennebury
Phoebe Adair Harris

Quilt label of *Nude Is Not a Color*
From the Collections of the Henry Ford

Back of *Nude Is Not a Color*
From the Collections of the Henry Ford

5/325 is likely unrecognizable to most, other than as a series of numbers. It is etched into my brain as the most common formulation of the prescription narcotic hydrocodone/acetaminophen I prescribe. With that number also comes the mixed benefits I regularly see with prescription narcotics, the people for whom it has spelled relief and those for whom it has spelled addiction. Supersizing those numbers, cutting them up, and mixing them back together in literal form tells of the mixed blessings.

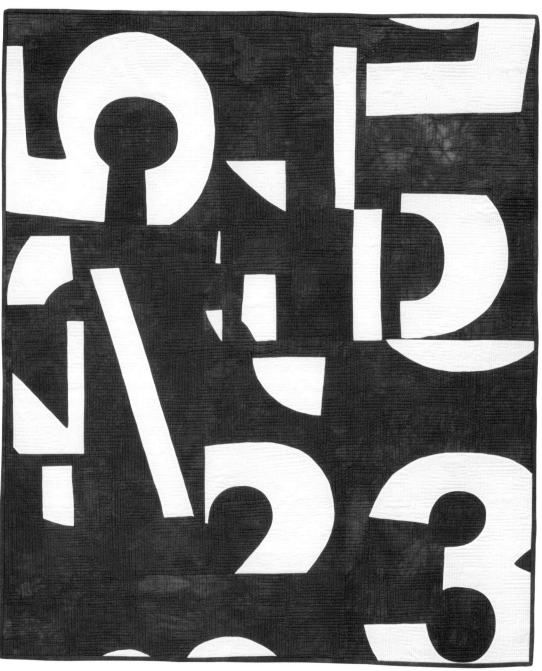

5/325, 60″ × 72″, 2015, designed, pieced, and quilted by Hillary Goodwin

ON
REVERSE

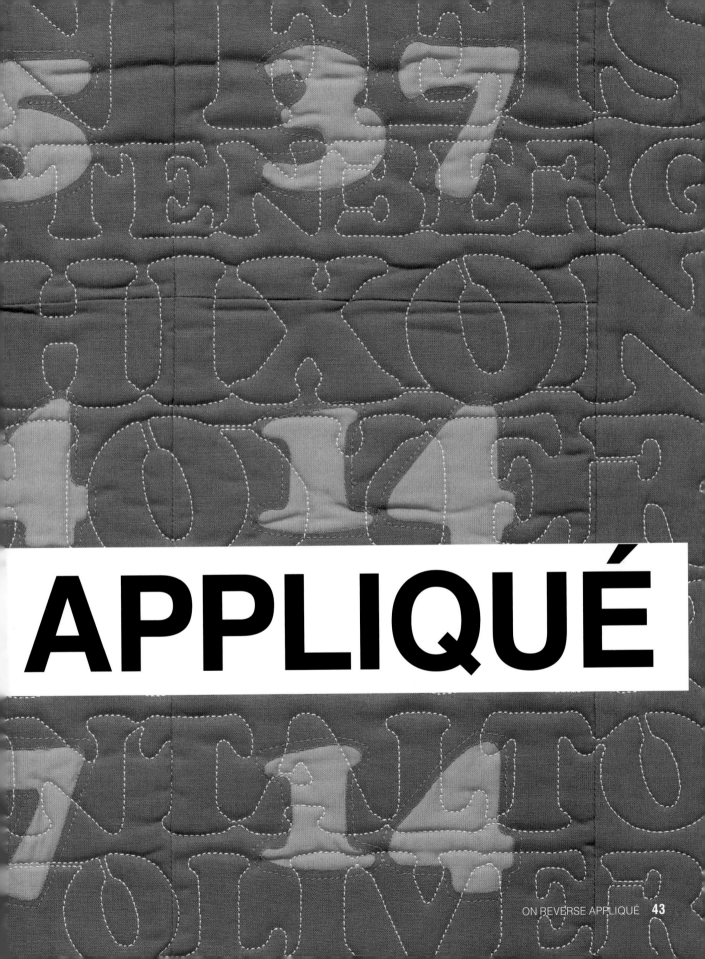

APPLIQUÉ

REVERSE APPLIQUÉ is, as one would suspect, the inverse of raw-edge appliqué.

Rather than cutting out letters to be stitched to a background, reverse appliqué involves carefully cutting letters out of the top layer and stitching fabric behind the resulting empty space. While raw-edge appliqué allows you to place letters wherever you wish with great ease, reverse appliqué requires a bit more planning. You can take as many tries as you need with standard appliqué, but once you cut into your base cloth for reverse appliqué, there is no going back.

Cutting out the letterforms is also a little more difficult than with basic appliqué; here you need to cut from the inside out, starting at the center of the letter and then making your way to the edges with your scissors. Straying outside of the boundaries of the letter may require beginning again with fresh cloth. Reverse appliqué leaves little room for error; precise scissor skills are required.

Just like with raw-edge appliqué, the process of reverse appliqué begins with tracing the letters you need onto a paper-backed fusible. And yes, the letters need to be reversed for the finished letterforms to be correct in the cloth. It is important to leave about an inch border around the letter or word, as that is what you are going to use to fuse the cloth backing that fills the negative-space letter. Next, fuse the traced letter to the back side of the base cloth, and carefully cut out the letter without straying outside the boundaries of the letterform.

At this point you're looking at a letter-shaped hole cut into your base cloth with the paper backing still on the fusible. Next, peel the paper backing from the fusible, and press the right side of the backing fabric to the base cloth. I usually cut my backing fabric a half-inch larger in all directions than the edge of the glue of the fusible; this way I easily avoid pressing my hot iron directly onto the fusible glue. Finally, flip the fabrics so that the base cloth is facing up, and stitch around the outside of the letterform—sewing in the base cloth, not the backing fabric. As with my standard appliqué, I aim to sew about $\frac{1}{16}$th of an inch from the edge of the letter.

Trace your reversed letter onto your paper-backed fusible such as Wonder-Under.

Iron your fusible with the letter to the wrong side of your base cloth.

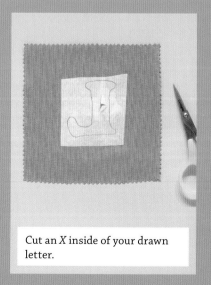
Cut an X inside of your drawn letter.

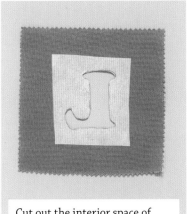

Cut out the interior space of your letter, leaving a letter-shaped hole in your fabric.

Carefully remove the paper backing from your fusible.

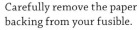

Iron your backing fabric to the fusible on the wrong side of your base cloth, making sure to completely cover the fusible glue.

Carefully stitch around the edge of your letter on your base cloth.

Reverse appliqué is a tad more involved than regular appliqué, but it has great benefits that make it an essential tool for making text-based quilts. The first advantage is that you can use fabric that is significantly lighter in color than the base cloth. Appliquéing white fabric to a black background will inevitably lead to seeing the base cloth right through the appliqué. With reverse appliqué, that problem is solved, and the full range of color possibilities opens up.

The second advantage lies entirely in the realm of subtle perception; reverse appliqué feels different than raw-edge appliqué even though both techniques leave a raw edge. Since the letterforms are no longer simply sitting on top of the base cloth, the viewer/reader ends up with a dual engagement of the letters and words. At first the letters pop to the foreground because that is where we are used to engaging letters—ink *on* paper, paint *on* canvas. It is a learned perceptual process born of years of experience. But then, on closer inspection, the viewer/reader sees that the letters are behind the base cloth, that the top layer has been incised, cut through, to reveal a second cloth that makes up the letters and words in the quilt.

The Right Tool for the Job

While you may be able to get away with using shears to cut out your letters for raw-edge appliqué, working from the inside to the boundary of the letterform will almost always necessitate a good pair of small sewing scissors.

Secrets

For this quilt that borrows a quotation from Poppy Z. Brite's book *Lost Souls*, I wanted a general feel of darkness, not the complete darkness of black but the dim light of a rich navy blue, something shy of pitch-black as though a single weakly glowing light cut ever so slightly through the darkness. I felt that this quilt should be a single tone on tone—a contrasting color would bring far too much vibrancy to 4 a.m. So my light blue letters sit behind the dark base cloth, readily visible without overly disturbing the general sensation of darkness.

In bringing the quotation, the limited color palette, and the technique of reverse appliqué together, I believe the resulting whole produces a sensation of being alone in the middle of the night. The color and design are intended to mirror the isolation and even depression implied in the quotation. That, ultimately, is the goal of working with a quotation: to visually translate it, to give it a form that reinforces the meaning rather than contradicts it.

Secrets, 60″ × 80″, 2022, designed and pieced by Thomas Knauer, quilted by Jennifer Strauser

IS THE HARDEST TIME TO BE ALIVE

AND 4AM KNOWS

Dreams

In this quilt, another, longer quotation is used, this time borrowed from A.A. Milne. While the previous quilt sought to evoke a somber mood, this quilt is intended to portray a joyful innocence. The letters are off-white behind a colorful array of base cloths, referencing a child's blocks. Again, reverse appliqué allows me to use the off-white for the letters to produce a continuity between them as well as a strong contrast between each block.

As you might guess, I like using quotations, fragments of existing texts, and found information in my quilts. So often, others have succinctly said what I want to convey. In borrowing text for my quilts, I feel like I am bringing something from the outside world into the intimate space of the quilt. This then creates a polyvocal object, entwining my voice as a quilter with the voice of the text's author. The quilt is simultaneously separable into its component parts and, ideally, uniquely complete as a single text/object. In the end, that is the real goal of any text-based quilt: to be visually taken apart, explored, and understood and then brought back together again.

Dreams, 62″ × 82″, 2022, designed and pieced by Thomas Knauer, quilted by Jennifer Strauser

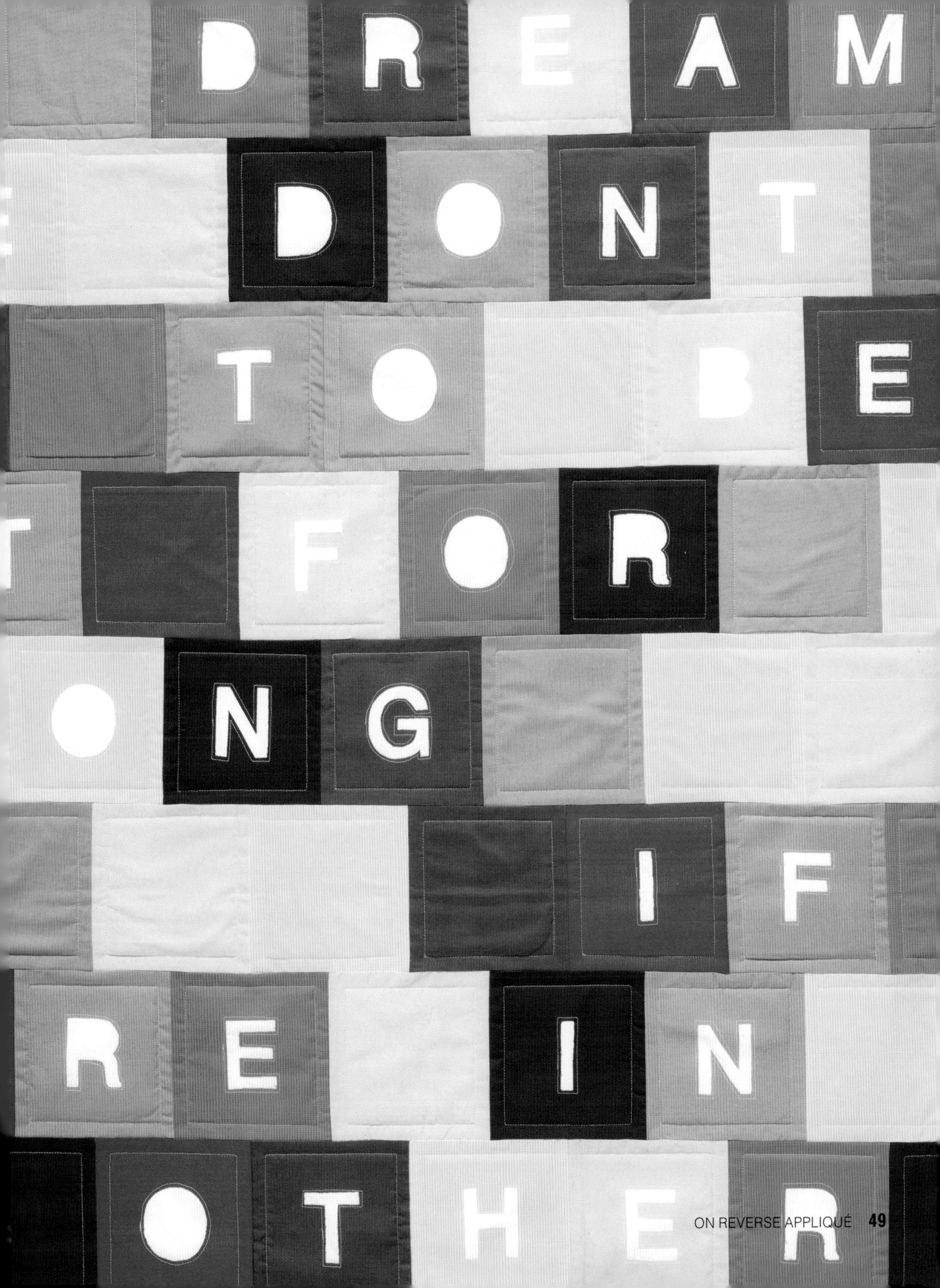
DREAM
DONT
TO BE
FOR
NG
IF
RE IN
OTHER

Numbers: Parkland

For this quilt there was never a real alternative to using reverse appliqué; concept and process seemed significantly connected. The numbers on this small quilt are the ages of the victims in the Parkland, Florida, mass shooting; they are cut into the base cloth as an irreparable incision. Each number stands for a life needlessly lost, tearing at the collective social fabric.

While standard appliqué speaks to me of the solidity of letters, reverse appliqué is based on a process of loss, losing the cloth that is cut away.

Here the quilting takes on a particular significance; this quilt is quilted with the names of the victims of that horrific day. I will write more specifically about using quilting as a means of adding text to a quilt, but for now, suffice it to say that the listing of the names and ages is meant to work in unison to create a small memorial, one that resides in my studio and serves as a reminder of why I make the type of quilt that I do.

Through these quilts, I hope that readers will come to see appliqué and reverse appliqué as unbelievably useful processes in the quilter's toolbox. Between the two approaches, any color and tone relationship can be handled successfully. The two approaches also bring a significant conceptual vocabulary for working with the material nature of text.

Numbers: Parkland, 22″ × 31¾″, 2018

ON
PIECED

LETTERS

With STANDARD APPLIQUÉ, letters are applied on top of the base cloth; with REVERSE APPLIQUÉ, the letters are cut out of the base cloth and then backed with another fabric.

Pieced lettering, on the other hand, works on a single layer of fabrics, piecing together a larger cloth rather than adding to or subtracting from it. As such, pieced lettering evokes traditional patchwork and takes on certain basic forms from the more general practice of piecing quilt tops to produce a final design.

In my practice, I use two types of pieced lettering. The first is paper piecing, in which a template is printed on paper; the fabric is sewn to that paper, carefully following the lines laid out on the pattern paper; and the paper is removed when the letter or block is completed. The second is simple patchwork piecing in which basic quilting shapes—squares, rectangles, half-square triangles—are brought together to form the different letters.

While I tend to use the two appliqué processes already covered, I appreciate the different visual sensibility of pieced letters. Pieced letters can be abstracted and almost hidden in a profusion of patchwork, taking on a dual role as both pure form and language. Even if just a few words are pieced into the quilt top, the piecing participates in this duality of language and form. Here the letters are embedded in the quilt rather than applied to it, producing a top that is formed of one layer. These quilts may be very traditional in their technique even as they are potentially subversive in their messages.

Accessing the Pieced Alphabet Template

As it's not necessarily easy to create an alphabet of pieced letters, I have prepared a pieced alphabet for you.

To access the pieced alphabet template, type the web address provided below into your browser window. tinyurl.com/11530-pattern2-download

ZUZANA PIECED ALPHABET

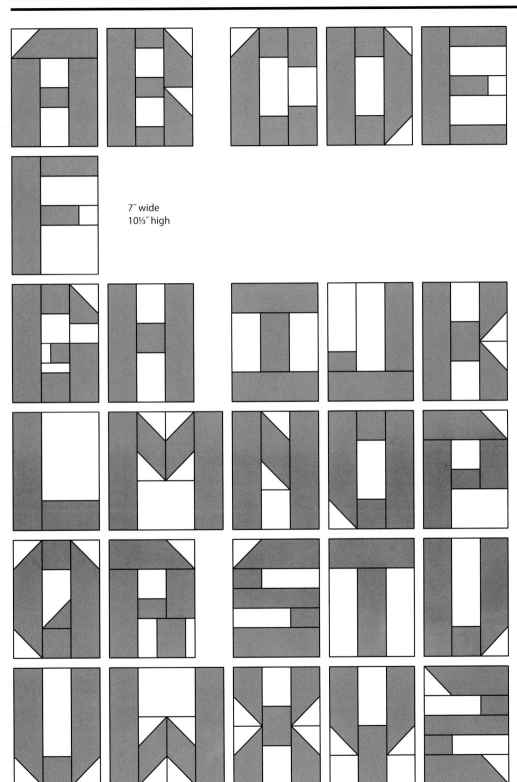

7˝ wide
10⅓˝ high

ME/YOU/US

This quilt is made using the paper-piecing method; each letter is highly abstracted in order to emphasize the patchwork and allow the lettering to be found upon further inspection. There are two blocks: One says "ME" and the other says "YOU." The quilt is a jumble of *ME*s and *YOU*s that add up to an *US*. It is an exploration of relationships in all their complexity.

Paper piecing allows me to produce highly unconventional letterforms without resorting to individual templates and tricky stitchery. With a little careful planning, just about any form can be achieved with paper piecing. With any paper-piecing project, I like to start by numbering the parts of my template to ensure I proceed in the proper/best order. To begin piecing, flip the template over so it is facing down; you will be working with the fabric on the back of the template and using the sewing lines on the front of the template to guide your stitching.

ME/YOU/US, 58½˝ × 58½˝, 2016
From the Handi Quilter Corporate Collection

Place a piece of fabric right side up over the back of the first numbered part of the template, and then add a second piece of fabric, right side down on top of the first. This piece will cover the second numbered part of the template; try to keep your piece of fabric relatively close to the size of the template space. Pin your fabrics to the template, flip the template over, and sew along the first sewing line. Flip the template back over to the fabric side, remove the pin(s), and press your second piece of fabric right side up, over template area two; the fabric should now be face up and fully covering template area two. Fold that fabric back over the first piece, fold your template along the line you just sewed, and trim both the first and second fabrics to ¼″ from the seam you just sewed. Then fold your template along the next stitching line, and trim the overhanging fabric to ¼″ from the stitching line. And there you go; repeat this process until you finish the template block, then trim ¼″ outside all four edges, and you're finished.

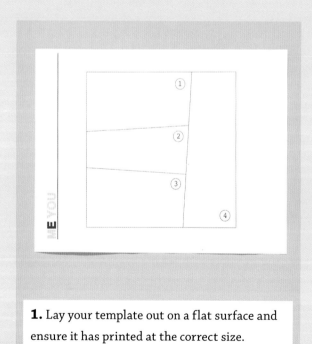

1. Lay your template out on a flat surface and ensure it has printed at the correct size.

2. Flip your template over, and place your first piece of fabric over your first section right side up. Be sure your fabric extends at least ¼″ beyond all of your stitching lines.

3. Place your second piece of fabric, wrong side up, on top of your first piece. Pin both pieces to your template.

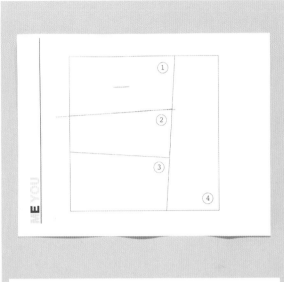

4. Flip your template over, and sew along your first stitching line.

5. Flip your template once again, and press the second piece of fabric so it is lying right side up.

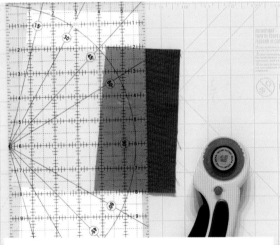

6. Fold that fabric back over the first piece, fold your template along the line you just sewed, and trim both the first and second fabrics to ¼″ from the seam you just sewed.

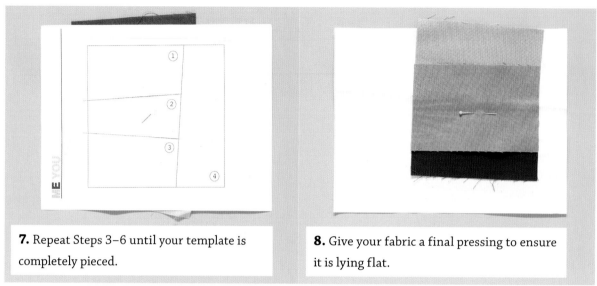

7. Repeat Steps 3–6 until your template is completely pieced.

8. Give your fabric a final pressing to ensure it is lying flat.

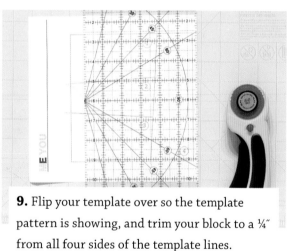

9. Flip your template over so the template pattern is showing, and trim your block to a ¼˝ from all four sides of the template lines.

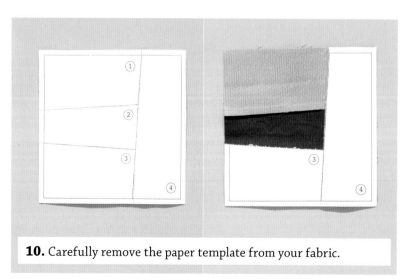

10. Carefully remove the paper template from your fabric.

11. Give your block a final pressing, and you're finished.

Make ME/YOU/US

SIZE: 58½″ × 58½″

This quilt takes advantage of an array of unconventional angles to create a top with a lot of movement even though it is made of only the two blocks: ME and YOU.

MATERIALS

APPROXIMATELY 7 YARDS OF
ASSORTED SCRAPS—the more scraps
the better

20 PAPER TEMPLATES OF EACH
LETTER: *Y, O, U, M,* and *E.* These are
available for download (see below)

BACKING: 4⅓ yards

BATTING: 73″ × 73″

BINDING: ⅝ yard

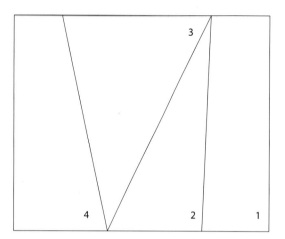

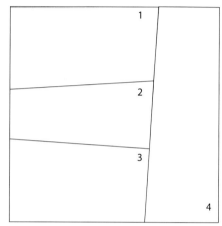

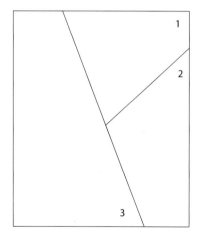

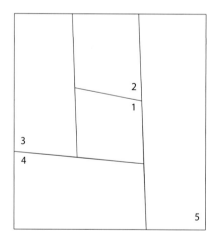

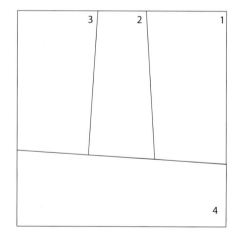

Accessing the ME/YOU/US Templates

To access the full-size templates, type the web
address provided below into your browser window.
tinyurl.com/11530-pattern3-download

Steps

Following the instructions for paper piecing *above*, make 20 versions of each letter. Create as much variety among the letters as possible.

Lay out your letters on your design wall or floor with each of 10 rows having 2 *YOU*s and 2 *ME*s, alternating which one goes first between lines—see diagram for guidance.

Once you have a layout you are happy with—this may take a bit of work—begin piecing your rows together.

When all of your rows are assembled, stitch your rows together until the quilt top is fully assembled.

Layer the top, batting, and backing; quilt as desired; and bind using your favorite method.

Not A Product

This quilt protests the commodification of quilts and quilting as the quilting industry has grown; it is a reminder that quilts are made with our hands, made with our labor, and given with love. It is a simple statement but one that I hope resonates. As more and more quilters are selling their work on Etsy or similar sites, some interesting conversations have emerged surrounding issues of commodification and value. This quilt refuses to participate in that space at all; it does not declare exactly what it is but instead rejects the idea of being a simple commodity.

I think there is something powerful about the negative assertion, the insistence on disallowing unwanted categorization. More and more, as I talk with guilds and individual quilters, I hear the question of value coming up, with quilters' wondering what a quilt is worth and how it compares in value to some other quilt. It is as though the twin powers of the quilting industry and the rise of online sites for selling handmade things have produced a monetization trap, one that gets us to reduce our labor, our skill, and our creativity to a dollar value, which warps the very notion of worth.

Not a Product, 80˝ × 80˝, 2022, designed and pieced by Thomas Knauer, quilted by Jennifer Strauser

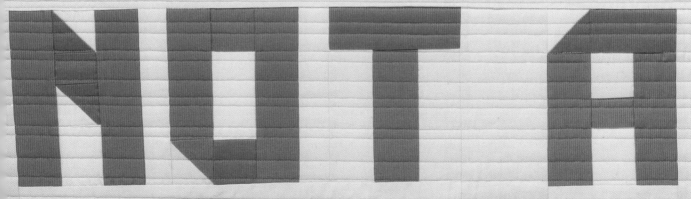

I would be remiss if I didn't mention one more approach to pieced letters: PIXELIZATION.

Here we eschew the idea of producing differing shapes to appropriately form a given letter and instead repeat a single shape—a square—to approximate the curves and angles of letters on a larger scale. My quilt *Ampersand* is an example of this, with the single typographic character formed across the entire surface of the quilt. I have taken the scale of this character to an extreme to emphatically assert the word *and*, which evokes an array of possible interpretations. Taken on a smaller scale, a good deal of text easily can be produced.

Thus we have yet another vocabulary of techniques and forms to produce text, and I hope we see the subtle, and not so subtle, differences that lend a unique voice to each of these approaches to working with text quilts. From here on out, we will be moving into less traditional approaches to creating text quilts, examining a wider array of language types and materials for making our words work.

Ampersand, 90˝ × 90˝, 2016, designed by Thomas Knauer, pieced by Rachael Gander, quilted by Lisa Sipes

Chawne Kimber /

So why put text on a quilt? Of course the answer is, Why not? But particularly, I was inspired by the words of Tonya Ricucci. Back in the early days of the internet, she was doing some improvisationally pieced lettering mainly to put names on quilts. And then she wrote a book, and in the examples in there, she had these four-letter-word quilts, and of course I kept expecting to see something different and hoping to see … I don't know, an honoring of the full English language. And instead, there were a lot of statements about hope and love. And all those are lovely, but I think that as long as we're censoring ourselves in this forum, we've got a big problem.

So I decided to make a quilt that sort of challenged that and then decided, "Well, okay, that's. …" It's cute to put slurs and other kinds of defamatory language on quilts, but really truly using the full English language is something that we ought to do. I think that we all should be able to explore full self-expression in a quilt. I got a little pushback on that back in the beginning, but I decided to keep pressing on, and people sort of liked what I was doing in a way that was not just titillating, like I got with my "fuck" quilts, but instead more relating to me as a person and the things that are important to me.

I think that the medium of the quilt is important for multiple reasons. One is that just the value of using something that's warm and associated with grandmothers and that has the connotation of truly protecting people is kind of a lovely juxtaposition to some of the commentaries that I'm trying to make about my life and about society. And so the quilt allows us to put those things together. It draws people in who appreciate the form of the quilt on a more utilitarian level and then starts to expand their horizons into the realm of art as they're asked to confront the … I don't know, the dichotomies that I'm trying to put before them.

For me, though, the quilt, especially made from cotton, is a reflection of my ancestry.

I do descend from people who were enslaved and who grew cotton involuntarily in the 1800s. To me, I don't think that you can talk about race in America without talking about cotton. And then we add in that my mother's descended from people who were enslaved and who grew rice and indigo. And so that brings us to my favorite combination, which is denim. Cotton things that have been drenched in indigo are absolutely the top choice for materials that I use in my work.

Hope Half Empty is made from denim and feed sacks, and the letters are pieced in the improvisational form. It is my own recipe for piecing letters that I adapted from the Tonya Ricucci book *Word Play Quilts*. The background is, of course, an improvisational pastiche of multiple shades of blue denim. The words "I miss hope" are kind of scrawled in a way as if it were just a note that someone needed to write to themselves in the middle of the night, admitting that they were going through a little bit of turmoil. For me, it comes out of a realization that I am middle-aged and recognizing that I don't have much more time here.

I have a little less hope because the future is not spreading out in front of me infinitely long. In the past, I used to be much more optimistic and used to think that there are more possibilities and that it's useful to keep trying at something. Whereas now, I calculate how much more time I have, how much more care I'm putting into things when instead I may want to double back and invest time in things that more clearly fill me up. I should say that this quilt is called *Hope Half Empty*. And so that filling up is the question that I'm trying to answer here. Hope Half Full would give you the sense that we're moving forward and that there's more hope to be gained, but over time, we all get worn down just from the evidence and the perspective that years on earth and knowing more people bring.

Hope Half Empty, 41″ × 48″, 2018, improvisationally machine pieced, hand quilted, and hand bound by Chawne Kimber

Detail of *Hope Half Empty* (see full quilt on page 69)

Hope Half Empty is a reflection on that, and it's also a quilt that I made in a political era in our nation that at least some people I know are not all that proud that we went through. And let's hope that it is not to return. The words on my quilt are also a reflection on missing the Obamas as our leaders. Those were some good years for some of us who really truly believe in human rights for all and progress in the nation. And that progress's being seated in value for human life and trust in each other. During Obama's elections, the words were all about hope and change, and boy, do I miss that hope that I had.

Cotton Sophisticate is a quilt that I finished in 2015, and it was actually motivated by the question of the labor stream that goes into the fabrics that we use. At the time, we had just seen the Rana Plaza tragedy in Bangladesh. A multistory sweatshop just collapsed in on itself, and all these workers who had been working for pennies making fast fashion for the Western world were basically decimated. We got to see firsthand the labor conditions that bring us much of our textile goods. And so I started ... well, I'd already started years before ... asking questions about the labor stream that goes into making the fresh yardage of quilting cottons that we buy from stores and then use to make our quilts.

Then this brand-new company, American Made Brand, came on the scene, and it uses cotton that's farmed in America. Then it manufactures the cotton into dyed fabric here in America. What that brings us is some guarantee that the work is being done under U.S. labor laws and, it is hoped, following those standards, and I choose to believe that they're following those standards. I was intrigued and really wanted to get involved with using these fabrics. When they first came out, the company had a little contest; use their fabrics and only their fabrics in a quilt and you could enter to be included in a small exhibition at the Houston International Quilt Festival. I didn't really need that motivation, but it was an interesting challenge. I of course bought every color available. I think there were 72, 75 colors; not sure. Not sure they had them all out there at the beginning, but I bought yardage of all of it. They didn't provide the yardage for the contest, but that's fine. I wanted to really use my money to support this company.

I embarked on making a hugely scrappy quilt, but without the words. I was just building those blocks and really having a lot of fun but realized that it was taking a long time, and there was no way I was going to make the deadline for this contest. And then I returned to these blocks and decided that I would use them to make an expressive quilt. I found I really wanted it to be something about choice and something about cotton. I just started looking around and remembered this quote, which is a summary sentence in Eartha Kitt's autobiography: "In essence, I am a sophisticated cotton picker." And in this, one finds a lot of meaning. So on the one hand, we take it at face value from her autobiography. Eartha Kitt was a quadruple threat, an actress, a dancer, a singer, and an all-around entertainer, and she was quite popular in the twentieth century, despite her race, despite her being a woman, and despite her not being a maternal sort of figure. She was really quite flamboyant and really kind of breaking the mold of what Black women had to be.

Cotton Sophisticate, 72″ × 72″, 2015, designed, pieced, and quilted by Chawne Kimber, machine quilting also by Pam Cole

But she grew up in the South, and like all Black kids in the South of a certain era, she had to take her turn picking some cotton. So in North Carolina, there in the threshing time, she would go out and pick balls of cotton. And this sentence is sort of a summary of her life. She started here in the cotton fields, and now look at this sophisticated woman that she became. She's never going to forget where she came from. And this is a statement that I reflect on quite a bit in thinking about my family history. No matter how many degrees we get, and no matter how high we climb on the ladders toward a certain flavor of success in this nation, African Americans can never escape this original sin of the nation of their ancestors having been enslaved. And so "In essence, I'm a sophisticated cotton picker" is actually something that we all strive for. And so I believe this is reflective of my own life and certainly the lives of my parents.

TEXT WITHOUT LETTERS

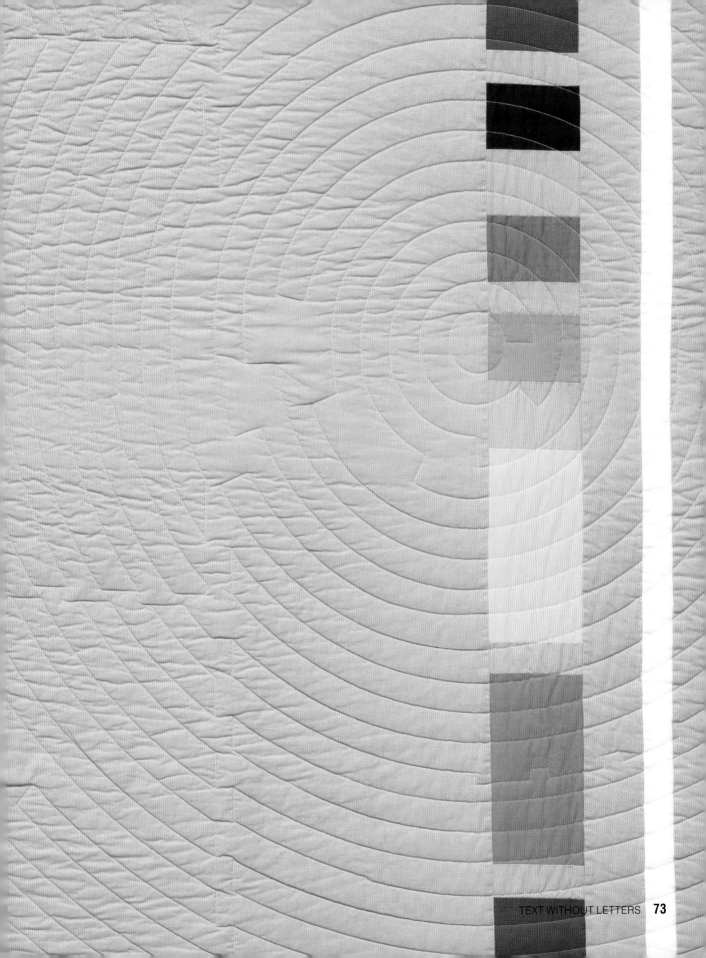

BEYOND working with various methods of getting letterforms onto my quilts, I use a range of alphabets.

Specifically, I really enjoy designing quilts using Morse code, Braille, and binary code. Each has its own visual vocabulary; together, they offer a wide variety of patchwork possibilities. And beyond the aesthetics of encoded quilts, there is something unique about the way these quilts speak; they contain secrets shared in little more than a whisper. They are quilts that only a few will have full access to; they are shared messages between friends and family.

I suppose that is the point of using encoded text: to create a closed circle, a privileged space that parcels out meaning bit by bit. At first look, these quilts seem to exist as pure patchwork: as abstraction, the play of color and shape. But then, perhaps, a pattern reveals itself and hints at an as-yet hidden message. And when the quilter shares the key to the code, possibly to only a few, this creates a further intimate bond between maker and recipient.

This intimacy of the secret text first drew me to making encoded quilts: I made quilts for family members that only they would understand. And for a while, these quilts remained secret messages. But over time I chose to share the keys to some of these quilts more widely, to allow outsiders into the circle.

Binary, Braille, and Morse code are methods of forming text without actually producing what we normally recognize as letters and words. Unlike straightforward text quilts, encoded quilts walk a fine line between communication and abstraction. These quilts play between the seemingly abstract pattern of the patchwork and the code that forms hidden letters. Because color changes, direction changes, and more can be both design tools and meaning makers in code quilts, their intersection of abstraction and language is unique among text quilts.

Smart Is Beautiful

Perhaps my favorite code quilt is the one I made for my daughter when she was about eight. I wanted to make her a quilt that would run counter to all of the messaging she was about to be bombarded with regarding beauty, what it is to be feminine, and ultimately what a woman should be. I wanted her to know, and be perpetually reminded, that her mind matters, that her thoughts are important, that smart is beautiful. But I couldn't just straightforwardly slap that text on a quilt and call it a day; the quilt needed to be smarter than that, subtler; text and form had to come together to create a larger message than the words alone.

Thus, *Smart Is Beautiful* was born. Each of the sixteen blocks stands for a letter as it would be depicted in binary code. Each white square can occupy one of two positions in its block, either left/right or up/down; this stood in for the binary of *0* and *1*. And so the words "smart is beautiful" are written into the quilt, hidden there just for her at first. In using a computer language to write my message, I was challenging her to see the world as multifaceted, to see that things can be more than they seem at first. It was also a reminder that she is profoundly beautiful beyond any aesthetic model, that she has a beautiful, brilliant mind that I love more than words could ever tell.

Smart Is Beautiful, 80˝ × 80˝, 2018

Binary Code

A	01000001	S	01010011
B	01000010	T	01010100
C	01000011	U	01010101
D	01000100	V	01010110
E	01000101	W	01010111
F	01000110	X	01011000
G	01000111	Y	01011001
H	01001000	Z	01011010
I	01001001	0	00110000
J	01001010	1	00110001
K	01001011	2	00110010
L	01001100	3	00110011
M	01001101	4	00110100
N	01001110	5	00110101
O	01001111	6	00110110
P	01010000	7	00110111
Q	01010001	8	00111000
R	01010010	9	00111001

Make Smart Is Beautiful

SIZE: 80″ × 80″ *This big, beautiful code quilt has an even bigger message.*

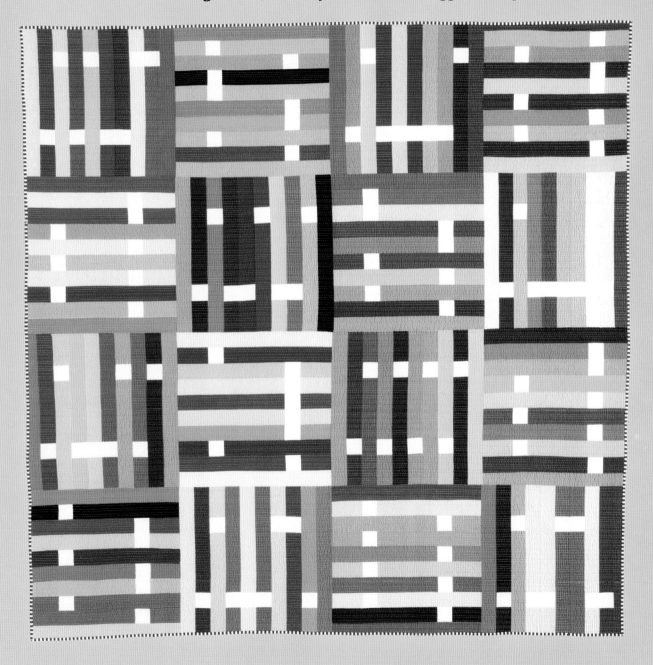

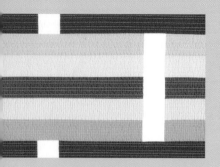

MATERIALS

⅔ YARD OF TEN COLORS OR PRINTS

⅔ YARD WHITE

BACKING: 7⅞ yards

BATTING: 88″ × 88″

BINDING: ¾ yard

CUTTING SIZES

A: 20.5″ × 2.5″ (various colors)

B: 14.5″ × 2.5″ (various colors)

C: 4.5″ × 2.5″ (various colors)

D: 2.5″ × 2.5″ (white)

Steps

Cut 2 A strips and 8 matching pairs of B and C strips for each block. You will also need 8 white D squares for each block.

Piece 8 central strips using 1 B strip, 1 D square, and 1 C strip each, making sure that the B and C fabrics match within each strip.

Assemble each set of ten strips (2 A and 8 B+C+D) according to the diagrams below and right, making sure each B+C+D strip is oriented in the correct direction.

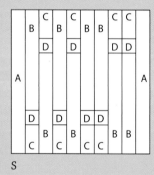

S

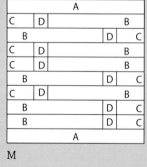

M

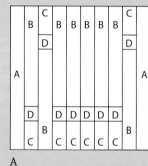

A

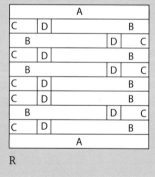

R

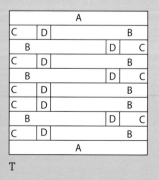

T

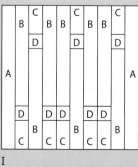

I

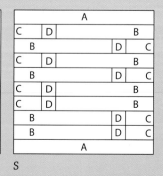

S

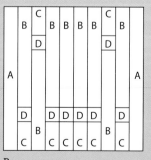

B

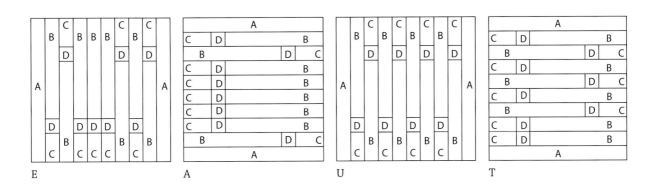

E   A   U   T

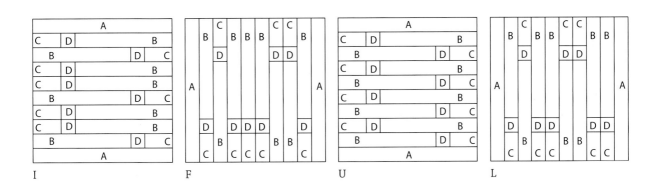

I   F   U   L

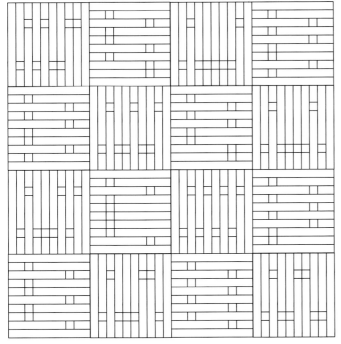

Repeat to make 16 blocks total.

Assemble your blocks, ensuring each is in the correct position.

Layer the top, batting, and backing; quilt as desired; and bind using your favorite method.

Morse Code

While binary code is almost infinitely flexible—*0* and *1* can be replaced by any visual duality—up/down, black/white, big/little, and so forth—Morse code is a little stricter and requires careful planning. The layout of the Morse code letters needs to be systematic, lest they devolve into a general mess. I usually form a consistent vertical axis, for example, by lining up a column of spaces between the dots and dashes.

For this quilt I vertically aligned one square from each Morse code letter block to create some degree of organization off of which the rest of the design could swing.

Characters in Morse Code

a	•–/	s	•••/
b	–•••/	t	–/
c	–•–•/	u	••–/
d	–••/	v	•••–/
e	•/	w	•––/
f	••–•/	x	–••–/
g	––•/	y	–•––/
h	••••/	z	––••/
i	••/	0	–––––/
j	•–––/	1	•––––/
k	–•–/	2	••–––/
l	•–••/	3	•••––/
m	––/	4	••••–/
n	–•/	5	•••••/
o	–––/	6	–••••/
p	•––•/	7	––•••/
q	––•–/	8	–––••/
r	•–•/	9	––––•/

Vows (Morse Code) is a quilt I made for my wife, wanting to explore the idea of a marriage quilt.

I translated the last line of our wedding vows—"and thereto I plight thee my troth"—into Morse code. You can see the prominent vertical axis between the yellow and orange elements. Each horizontal grouping is a single letter despite the color play, and the letters read down the quilt. Ultimately, Morse code is just a series of squares and rectangles and can be manipulated and played with in countless ways. So while the specific patterns of dots and dashes may be a little more constraining than the simplicity of binary code, there is still a great deal of room for visual experimentation.

With this quilt I was intrigued by the idea of literally stitching our vows into the fabric of a quilt and making them a part of our daily life. So not only are our vows spelled out in the piecing of the Morse code, but our complete wedding vows were translated into Morse code and developed into something like a Morse code stipple for the final computerized quilting process. Each line of quilting is broken up by short and long deviations from the would-be straight line. The short and long represent dots and dashes, and our vows become the texture of the quilt.

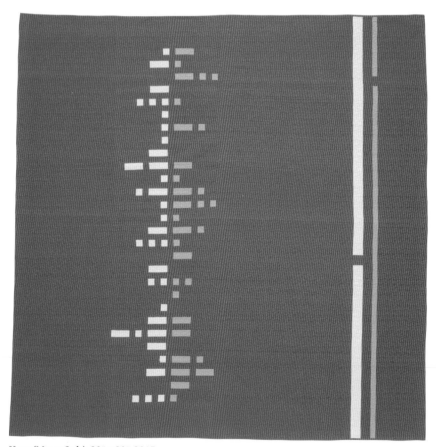

Vows (Morse Code), 80˝ × 80˝, 2015

Troth (Pride)

This quilt begins with the word *troth* from the wedding vows in the original Book of Common Prayer. The word itself was chosen because of its meaning: faith or loyalty. Rather than simply appliqué the word onto the quilt, I translated the word *troth* into Morse code and pieced it vertically down the middle of the quilt, using the colors of the pride flag. I hoped that by joining the pride flag with this fragment of the wedding vows, I could make a statement about the normality of same-sex marriages in the face of a country that is so often inhospitable to the LGBTQ+ community. In linking the pride flag to the concepts of faith and loyalty, I hoped viewers would focus on the essential elements of any marriage and in doing so equalize all marriages.

Troth (Pride), 80˝ × 80˝, 2015

Do Wrong to None

Finally, we have Braille, which is definitely the strictest of the visual alphabets that I use. Each letter is formed by a six-block unit (two columns of three blocks), with each block representing a bump in the paper or a flat area that goes into the composing of Braille for reading. While the overall form cannot be changed, there is a great deal of room for play in how each of the six blocks in a letter is handled. In my quilt *Do Wrong to None*, which I made for my son, color differentiates between a bump/dot and a flat/blank space: red half-square triangles denote dots, and yellow half-square triangles represent flat spaces. Each block of six forms a letter to spell out the Shakespeare quotation "Love all, trust a few, do wrong to none."

Braille

a	b	c	d	e	f	g	h	i	j

k	l	m	n	o	p	q	r	s	t

u	v	w	x	y	z	0	1	2	3

4	5	6	7	8	9

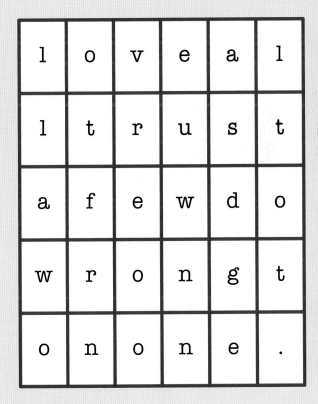

l	o	v	e	a	l
l	t	r	u	s	t
a	f	e	w	d	o
w	r	o	n	g	t
o	n	o	n	e	.

As you can see, the half-square triangles allow me to form a larger diamond-in-diamond pattern (with deviations) for the overall design of the quilt. Since Braille is fundamentally block based, there are all kinds of opportunities for developing unique visual relationships while still following the rules of Braille lettering. Again, any either/or relationship can work, with dots represented one way and blanks another. Handled thoughtfully, one can develop wonderful allover designs while still privately conveying a message.

Ultimately, all of these methods of adding encoded text to a quilt come down to either/or relationships: the 0/1 of binary, the dots and dashes of Morse, and the dots and blanks of Braille. Unlike other text quilts, the letters and words become materials for design exploration and color play. Yes, the design is constrained by preexisting forms for each letter, but this is not an imposing constraint. Every encoded quilt is a balancing act between aesthetic possibilities and the encoded letterforms themselves. It is this balancing act that opens a space for extraordinary design while maintaining the meaning of the text itself.

Do Wrong to None, 60″ × 74½″, 2019, designed and pieced by Thomas Knauer, quilted by Jennifer Strauser

Alexis Diese

I write for a living and have always been drawn to artwork that incorporates text, especially the work of Jenny Holzer, Barbara Kruger, Adrian Piper, and Christopher Wool, whose large painting "Terrorist"—after hanging without much notice in the Baltimore Museum of Art since it was made in the 1980s—suddenly ignited a controversy in the aftermath of 9/11 and was a particular source of inspiration for this quilt.

Text, words, and language are such powerful tools of communication that carry connotations from unmistakable to opaque, so the choice of words can generate a powerful punch of meaning that few other expressive choices can.

In turn, the use of a quilt as an expressive medium creates inescapable associations for the viewer; we are all touching and experiencing textiles from the moment we are born. The viewer of a quilt, therefore, feels an immediate visceral connection to the artwork based on its form, even before considering its composition and other features. To put it another way, the quilt comes "preloaded" with meaning.

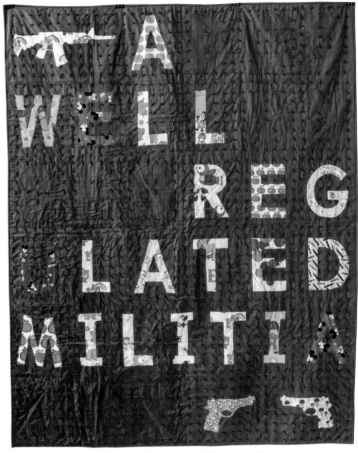

Comfort Quilt for a Lockdown Drill, 60″ × 72″, 2018, designed by Alexis Deise, pieced (hand appliquéd and machine pieced) by Alexis Deise, quilted (hand tied) by Alexis Deise

Because meaning already resides in the medium, the application of carefully chosen text can be layered on top of that meaning, resulting in an incredibly expressive message. With this quilt, some standard quilting conventions such as the use of juvenile fabrics and sheetings, appliqué, and brightly colored yarn ties invoke the comfort and innocence of childhood, contrasting with the text, a phrase from the Second Amendment often omitted in discussions of the "right to bear arms": together, quilt and text combine to ask us to consider what we are expecting children to sacrifice or become in service to our national obsession with guns.

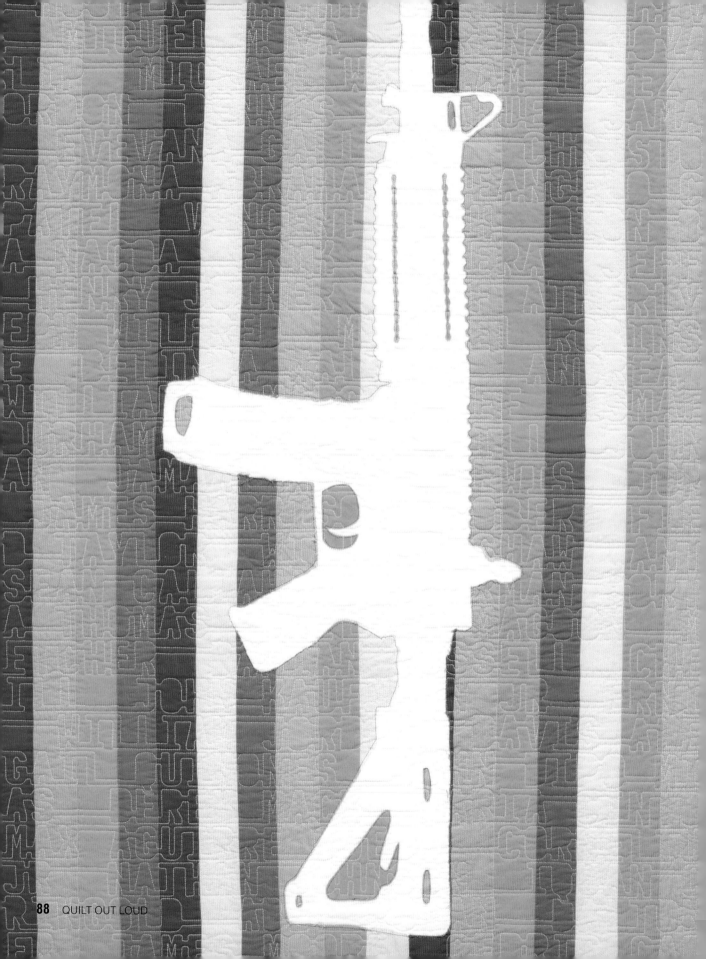

STITCHING

OUT

LOUD

THUS FAR, the book has focused on ways of using fabric to get text onto quilts.

While these approaches offer an abundance of possibilities, there is another method that has yet to be discussed: quilting your text into the quilt. Quilting the text directly into a quilt allows a second voice to emerge, one that does not necessarily follow what is pieced in or appliquéd onto the quilt top. The two voices may agree or be in conflict, but either way, a certain synergy occurs when developing this second quilting voice.

In my practice I have largely used a computerized longarm, designing my text in Adobe Illustrator and importing it to be converted to a file format the longarm understands. This is a highly complicated method and really works for only those with some advanced design skills. Fortunately, there are some workarounds that facilitate quilting with text.

The first, and easiest, way to quilt with text is to use your own handwriting on a longarm or by free-motion quilting on your domestic machine. It will take some practice as some letters (such as *t*) need to be drawn differently than one would with pen and paper; stopping to cross each and every *t* just isn't feasible. That said, with a little practice, using handwriting for quilting will flow as easily as any other quilting design that you're comfortable with.

Another method is to design your own pantographs for longarming. For this method, I split my letters into an upper part and a lower part, with the upper part stitched left to right and the bottom half coming back right to left. First, I draw two parallel lines across the width of my paper. Next, I lay that piece of paper over the printed text that I wish to convert to stitching. Just like with appliqué, I outline each letter, making sure the parallel lines pass through each letter. One could leave that pretty much as it is, but the sole pair of lines running through the text will inevitably create some awkward transitions. So to fix that, I pick alternate placements for the lines between letters to minimize the visual disruption. Finally, I erase any unnecessary lines, and my basic pantograph is ready. This process can be repeated as many times as needed to add more text, with each part of the overall design taped together to produce the final pantograph. Ultimately, I make use of a mix of all these techniques as needed, selecting the method that best fits the need.

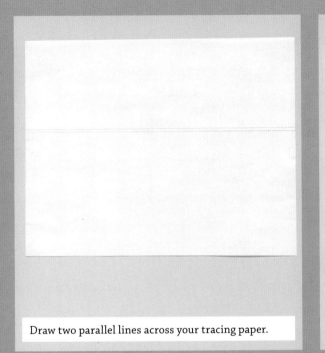

Draw two parallel lines across your tracing paper.

Lay your tracing paper over the word you want to make into a pantograph with the two lines running through the center of the letters and trace each letter.

Add connections between letters where they are closest to each other.

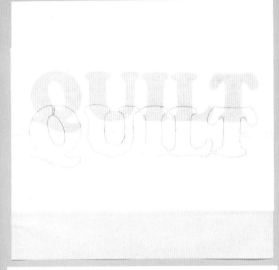

Erase all excess lines, leaving one continuous line across the top and one across the bottom. This is your pantograph.

Tea and Skittles

Tea and Skittles is a memorial quilt for Trayvon Martin; the appliqué is based on a shooting range target that was produced and sold after the killing of this young man. For the quilting, I used a computerized longarm to stitch in an excerpt from his obituary, a piece of text that showed extraordinary grace from Trayvon's family as it asked the community and country to come together to make sure something like this could never happen again. (Unfortunately, we have failed to act on that call.) In combining the voice of the appliqué with the voice of the quilting, a more complex whole is formed, one that simultaneously elicits anger and solidarity, sadness and a glimmer of hope.

Tea and Skittles, 48″ × 40″, 2016, from the Collections of the Henry Ford

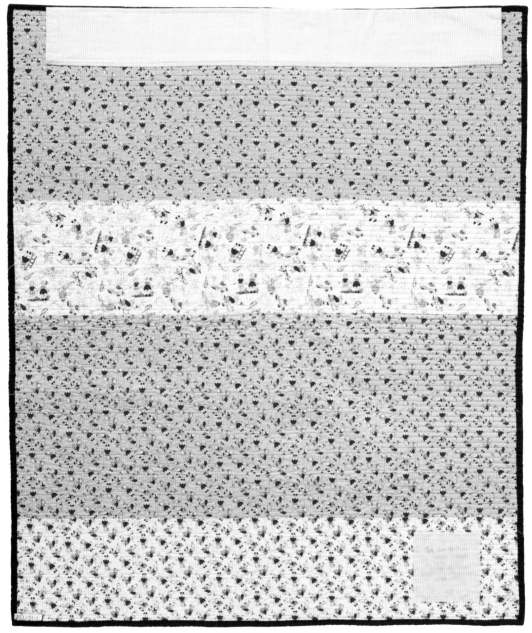

Back of *Tea and Skittles*

Now I Lay Me Down to Sleep

This quilt is a double quilt, split between a space under which a person would presumably sleep and a space for a detailed, reverse appliquéd AR-15 rifle. The obvious implication is that the second person is missing due to yet another shooting, another occurrence of gun violence. For the quilting, I again used a computerized longarm to stitch in the names of scores of victims of gun violence, a fragment of a seemingly never-ending list. Here the quilting reinforces the piecing and reverse appliqué, forcing the viewer to confront the enormity of the gun violence epidemic in America.

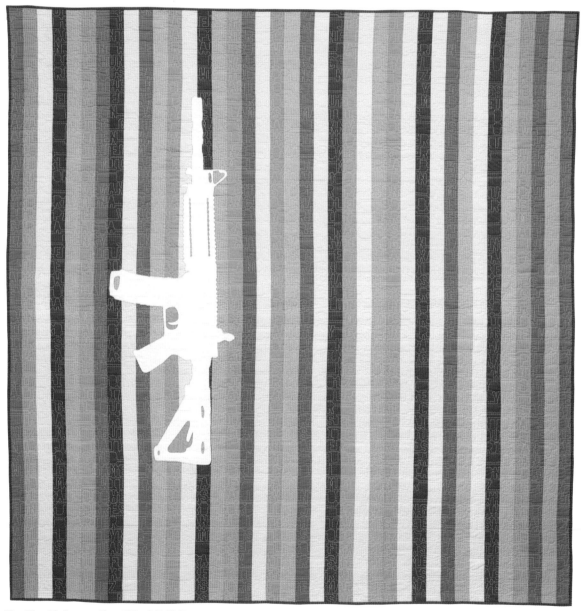

Now I Lay Me Down to Sleep, 74″ × 74″, 2018

Your Heritage Is Written in Other People's Blood

The efforts by some in this country to separate the meaning of the Confederate battle flag from its historic significance is nothing less than an attempt to whitewash history. Claiming that it stands for Southern pride leaves out what that flag meant 160 years ago and what it has been connected to since: the Ku Klux Klan and an ever-growing number of White supremacist groups. The initial experience of this quilt, made from pieced-together Confederate rally flags, is that of an abstract pattern; it reveals its constituent parts only after scrutiny. What was initially obscure hits the viewer with the force of this terrible symbol. Furthermore, the quilt is stitched with the names of both lynching victims from historical records and African American men and children killed in recent years. As such, this quilt sets out to resist racist attempts to rebrand the Confederate flag as a point of pride and instead ties it inextricably to its own true history. Ultimately, this quilt is about the tangible connection of symbols and their implications and the hostility implicit in using an iconography of violence.

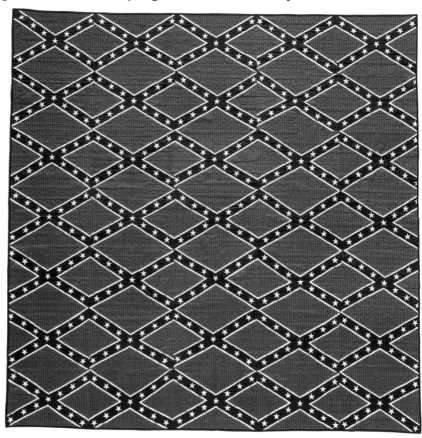

Your Heritage Is Written in Other People's Blood, 74″ × 74″, 2018

Chronic: I'm Tired of Being Sick

This seemingly simple quilt is made of a vintage twin bedsheet quilted with a single phrase repeated across the entirety of the quilt. What makes it complicated is that the quilting in my own handwriting repeats the phrase "i am tired of being sick." This then becomes an exploration and demonstration of life with chronic illness. The repetition takes on a profound weight as it is said over and over again, only once stitched in black rather than white to make the text readable.

Chronic: I'm Tired of Being Sick, 60˝ × 80˝, 2016

iamtiredofbeingsick

It Takes a Million Stitches to Tell You How Much I Love You

Though the piecing and reverse appliqué of this are simple—the dots spell out the word *plight* in braille, from the final line of our wedding vows ("and thereto I plight thee my troth")—the quilting is perhaps the most involved I have ever done. The entire surface of the quilt is stitched with our complete wedding vows in one-inch letters; quilting it took literally a million stitches (and a little more). Like the Morse code quilt with our vows from the previous chapter, in stitching our wedding vows into the fabric of the quilt, I am making a symbolic gesture toward making our wedding vows a part of our everyday.

So quilting with text can readily offer a second voice for a quilt, often unnoticed at first. It can take on a wide range of tones: Smaller lettering almost takes the place of a stipple; larger lettering can make a bold statement. But here the text becomes texture, embedding itself in a quilt, present but more ethereal than fabric lettering as its delicate line winds its way across a quilt.

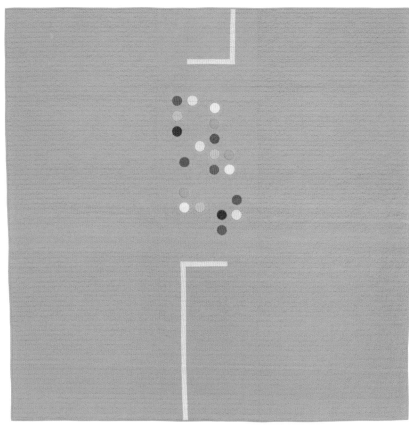

It Takes a Million Stitches to Tell You How Much I Love You, 80″ × 80″, 2015

Molli Sparkles

When I began my quilting journey, I never anticipated incorporating text into my quilts. However, as I hand embroidered a special message to my grandmother on the backside of my first quilt, I suddenly knew there was abundant opportunity. I had previously used words and prose throughout my creative life—as an author and a photographer—but now any words I chose to incorporate would be imbued with even greater meaning. They could be seen and touched, and most important, they could be felt in every sense of the word. This realization allowed me to see that a quilt's message could be reinforced or focused by textual motifs.

Words have always mattered to me. They've allowed me to convey intimate thoughts, humorous musings, and esoteric diatribes. Writing the story of a quilt is just as important to me as the quilt itself. I want people to hear the voice of the quilt, in the same way that it speaks to me when it is in the infancy of creation. I ensure I document these stories for every quilt on my website, but clearly, that information is not available to every viewer. Instead, text on a quilt can lead the audience to the archetypes I'm presenting through the work. Even a single word sewn into the quilt can provide enough context for viewers to make their own inferences about my larger intentions.

In addition, I adore double entendres, turns of phrase, and satirical irony. Incorporating textual applications of any of these into a quilt is the wadding that keeps me warm at night! As quilts are typically seen as a traditional, innocuous craft, combining them with unexpected words and phrases can lead to more subversive interpretations. Quilts don't have to be pretty and precious, and using text in combination provides the opportunity to negate those expectations. There's nothing better for me than engaging the viewer in a bit of tongue-in-cheek wordplay!

For instance, *No Value Does Not Equal Free* speaks to the economics of quilting, but it also pays homage to the all-white fabrics, devoid of any perceived color value. The dichotomy of the title was important to express through the quilting so that the viewer had a reason to investigate the quilt further. These titular words are intended to emerge only for those willing to invest the time looking for them. Time is money, and while this quilt measures both concepts, it is the use of text as both an entry and exit point of the design that allows for that discovery.

The engagement of text on my quilts is fluid, in the same way that language is ever changing. Whether it is the sparse words of a quilt label or the running prose that dances across an entire quilt, text is an aspirational element. Each interpretation of the words will be different, and as an artist, I can only hope that people will read between the lines.

No Value Does Not Equal Free, 72″ × 72″, 2014, designed and pieced by Molli Sparkles, quilted by Jane Davidson

SEEING THE DATA

Thus far, each chapter has covered a different method for adding text to quilts, but in this chapter, I would like to look at a special category of communication that is uniquely suited to quiltmaking:

DATA VISUALIZATION.

While data visualization can sometimes simply use numbers and letters to convey the intended information, more often than not, a careful deployment of interrelated shapes represents and communicates the information at hand.

Pie charts, bar graphs, and scatter plots are all examples of data visualization. Each wedge of a pie chart represents a certain percentage of the whole. Bar graphs allow the easy comparison of elements through the use of scale, and scatter plots present the relative positions of elements on a mathematical grid.

Data visualization can be a powerful method of communicating complex ideas and scales too large to really comprehend simply as numerical data. At its best, data visualization takes complex sets of data and renders them understandable through the use of visual devices. There is a reason the ubiquitous pie chart is still used: It works. It can tell the complex story of interrelated things in a simple graphic. The same holds for the array of charts and graphs we are so accustomed to seeing: They function effectively precisely because we are used to them. The medium, when used properly, illuminates the data rather than obscures it. The shapes and colors bring life to a list of numbers and ideally enhance and amplify the meaning held in the data.

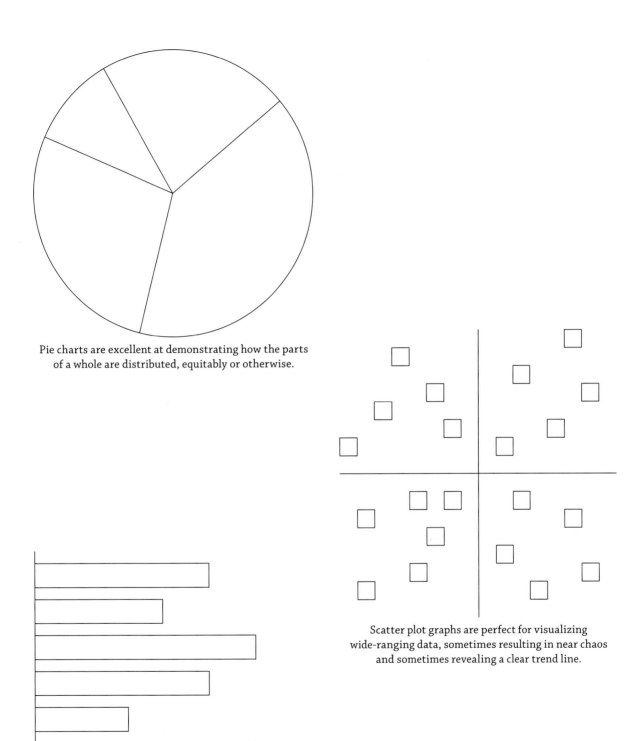

Pie charts are excellent at demonstrating how the parts of a whole are distributed, equitably or otherwise.

Scatter plot graphs are perfect for visualizing wide-ranging data, sometimes resulting in near chaos and sometimes revealing a clear trend line.

Bar graphs excel in demonstrating differences between elements or changes in one element over time.

COVID: 11–17 October 2021

Of course there are exceptions; sometimes the numbers just speak for themselves. In *COVID: 11–17 October 2021*, I simply listed the cumulative death toll of COVID for each day of a single week. The scale of the numbers is overwhelming and illustrates the brutality of COVID's death toll. Here the list of numbers serves as the simplest form of data visualization; the relatively short length of the data set allows it to be comprehensible without turning to abstract form to communicate the information.

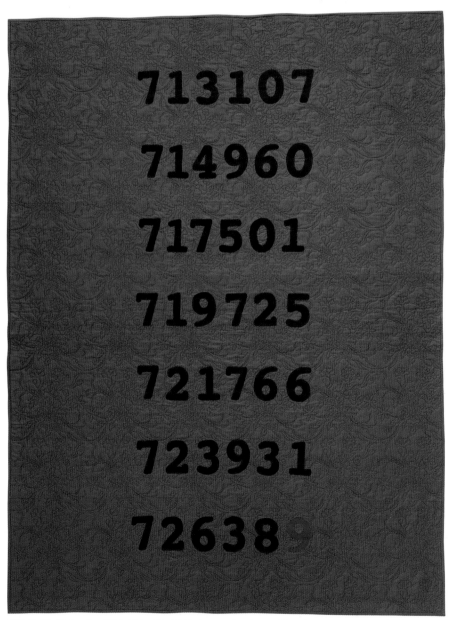

COVID: 11–17 October 2021, 60˝ × 80˝, 2022, designed and pieced by Thomas Knauer, quilted by Jennifer Strauser

9725

1766

3931

6389

Pie Charts

In my quilt *Pie Charts*, sixteen pie charts illustrate the income distribution of various G20 nations. Each color in the pie chart represents the gross income of one quintile (20%) of the population. From blue (the top quintile) to purple, to red, to orange, to green (the bottom quintile), the pie chart represents each quintile of a nation's income. While it's possible to compare the pie charts, they resemble each other closely: It becomes apparent that the blue part of the chart occupies an overwhelming proportion of the space, illustrating the concentration of income in the top quintile of each nation's population. The United States is set on a white background to bring it into focus, and that block is quilted with a quotation from Martin Luther King Jr.'s Nobel Prize acceptance speech, in which he likened income inequality to cannibalism.

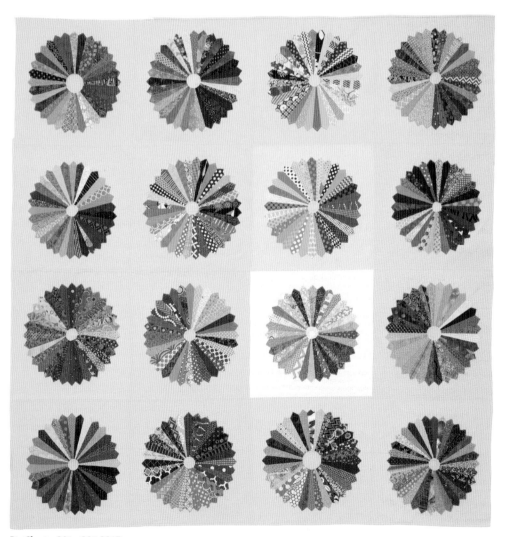

Pie Charts, 80″ × 80″, 2017

Excess

On average, approximately 1,600 people die in incidents of domestic violence each year. Thus the quilt *Excess* is composed of 1,600 small blocks, each of which represents one of those deaths. The blocks are divided between red/orange and blue/green. The color division illustrates the rates of death of women and men, with 80% of the deaths being women's. While the quilt's design represents the quantity and distribution of the tragic deaths, its scale may be its most important feature. Rather than producing a quilt in traditional bed-quilt dimensions, this quilt is 40″ wide and 160″ long so that when hung, fold after fold of the quilt lies on the floor. The quilt is in excess of the wall space, just as each of these deaths is a tragic excess. Here the enormity of death comes across both through the shear mass of 1,600 blocks and through the excessive length of the quilt as a whole.

Excess, 40″ × 160″, 2014, designed by Thomas Knauer, pieced with the help of many hands, quilted by Lisa Sipes

Data visualization can be a powerful communicative tool that is not always linguistic in nature but always resides in a place adjacent to language. Used well, data visualization can communicate a large quantity of numbers or words: data sets that are beyond easy comprehension unless transformed into a visual/symbolic form. And within the realm of quilting there is enormous potential for playing with pattern and color to create these graphs and charts, to bring them to vivid life, to invoke a double reality of information and aesthetics.

Heidi Parkes

I became a quilter in 2013, a very difficult year for me and the first time that I ever saw a therapist. I found, and continue to find, implicit comfort in quilts and handwork, which has infused a tender, meaningful, diaristic quality in my art.

The collective energy in the Threads of Resistance exhibition appealed to me after the 2016 election, sourcing comfort both in textiles and in community. I knit pink hats for my dad and stepmom, and we attended the Wisconsin Women's March. The "other side" was a confounding place, but in conversations with my dear friends, I discovered that we all knew and loved people who had voted for something that made us cry in grief. For me, it was a shift in my mom's politics, in sync with her move from Illinois to Florida. I was beginning to feel numb to the divisiveness, Facebook posts, and march posters, so I tried a pivot: aiming to create a quilt containing something vulnerable and soft that I hoped might be listened to.

I started with a curtain from IKEA that my mom had hand hemmed for me: physical proof of her love. Only later did I realize the perfection of a curtain, the barrier between public and private. Next, I set to work with a yellow notepad, handwriting more than 50 phrases that might fit my subject. I cut them into thin strips and laid them on my floor alongside the curtain. The process of hand embroidering gave me lots of time between words and phrases, and it allowed me to consider bold and subtle colors, forms of handwriting, and scale. Beneath the curtain, I unfurled black thread, a gesture of immediacy, that connected with the tangle of knots I felt in my stomach.

I'd lived with my mom until I was 30, and when I moved out, she hemmed that curtain for my new home. It was tough having our close relationship relegated to phone and email after her move south, and I palpably felt a physical and ideological space growing between us. I adore my mom and see her as a role model for the self-employed life that I've built as a quilter. Trusting her insights and advice had been second nature for me, and this rift stirred questions about integrity and our ability to share about other life topics too. Unable to force a conversation with her, I had a conversation with the quilt instead. When it was accepted into the traveling exhibition, however, I had a throat chakra event. Within a day of my acceptance letter, I had a terrible sore throat and cold; I knew I had to find a way to tell my mom about the quilt before she saw it on social media. That was the first moment that I was able to pierce through the silence into a dialogue.

Now, five years and many conversations later, this quilt that helped me find my words has opened lines of communication in my family. The text is visually challenging to read, and there's a slowing down as people digest it. In seeing folks from both sides of the aisle with *There's Something Between Us*, the way it fills their eyes with tears just like mine, I think there's a magic in what cloth, hand, and text can break open.

The text on my quilt:

My mother voted for a man who bragged about
non-consensually groping young women like me.
My grandma says, never talk politics with family.
If we can't talk about this,
how can we talk about anything else.
What else will she look past?
← *Right here ... my mom hemmed these curtains for me in 2013.*
But in 2016 she voted for me to lose my healthcare.
I voted like my neighbors,
and my mom voted like her neighbors.

There's Something Between Us, 56″ × 38″, 2017, Heidi Parkes

ON

MORE

POSSIBILITIES

THUS FAR, this book has covered some of the more conventional methods of producing text quilts. In this chapter I would like to explore some of the other possibilities, as there is a wide array of tools at our disposal. Some remain firmly within the quilting universe, while others push the boundaries of bed quilts and dive directly into the realm of art quilts.

When I need text that is smaller than can be reasonably appliquéd, I frequently turn to Spoonflower to print my text directly onto cloth. This approach allows for all manner of difficult arrangements, an endless range of scale, and the ability to select just the right color or pattern. This printed text can be incorporated into a larger pieced quilt—such as blocks of text interspersed with pieced blocks—or the printed cloth can be the entirety of the quilt top, as in the small quilt I had printed for my daughter.

Rabbit, 40″ × 50″, 2022, designed by Thomas Knauer, quilted by Jennifer Strauser

RABBIT

any of a family
of long-eared
short-tailed
lagomorph
mammals
with long
hind
legs

ANOTHER METHOD that holds great potential is embroidering text onto the quilt top.

This handwork evokes a certain intimacy; the letters stand out more than with quilted text but still allow for minute writing. Embroidered text on a quilt somehow feels like diary writing to me, creating a private text that we as viewers have come across. This is especially true with some of Heidi Parkes's quilts, in which the embroidered text gives us a peek inside a private conversation.

Of course, there is always needle-turn appliqué, but I find that extraordinarily unwieldy for angular letters.

It is possible, but I find it to be a technique of diminishing returns when it comes to letterforms, especially when fused raw-edge appliqué offers such excellent results. But there are some very curvy fonts out there—such as Cooper Black—that would make needle-turn a whole lot more manageable; it is just a matter of selecting your fonts carefully.

Beyond these more conventional approaches, there are myriad possibilities available for applying text to a quilt. Iron-on letters are always an option, and fabric paints or fabric markers offer an extremely immediate technique for forming your letters. With paints and markers—and crayons/pastels—letters can be carefully drawn or wildly scrawled. While some of these materials don't lend themselves to bed quilts, they do allow for an enormous range of styles, producing a panoply of potential emotional responses.

So if you are looking for something out of the ordinary, there are plenty of options out there for producing extraordinary text. It is simply a matter of fitting the medium to the message, the application to the intended emotions. Going beyond the traditional eliminates any impediments to making text-based quilts. All you need is something to say and some experimentation to find your unique voice.

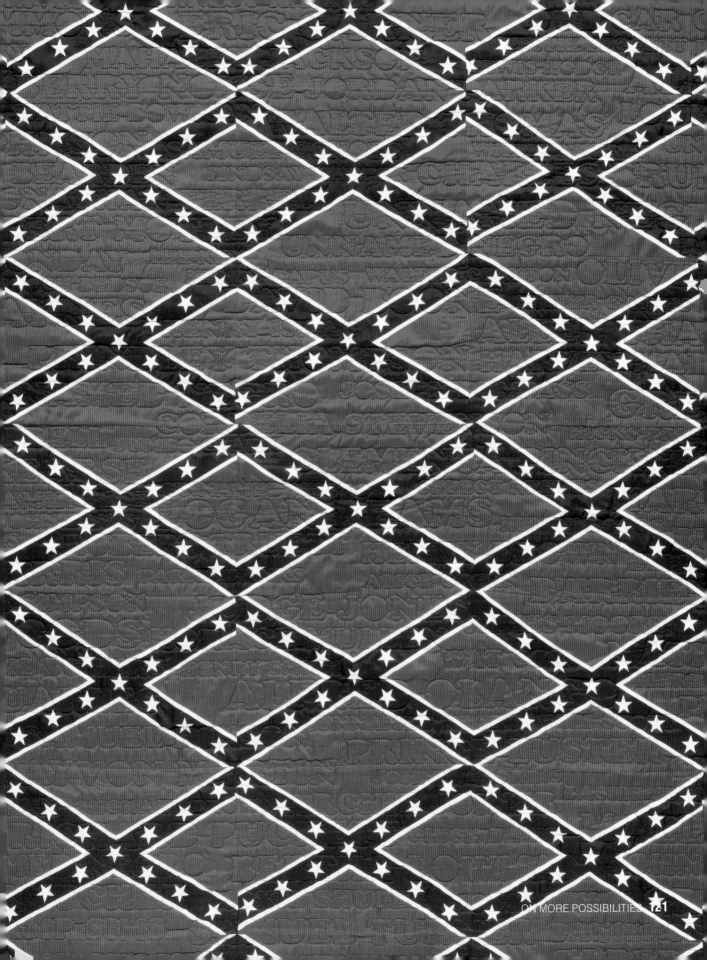

THE CALLER T[...]
THE GUN WAS [...]

WORKING

CE SAID THAT
OBABLY FAKE

IN
SERIES

I have been working in series almost from the beginning of my practice as an ARTIST.

At first, the quilts were aesthetic variations, exploring just what I could do with fabric and thread. But very soon the idea of a series became part of a conceptual practice, a framework for telling big stories.

Quilts in a series can speak individually and at the same time tell a larger story. The series takes pressure off the individual quilt, allowing it to speak succinctly, while forming greater meaning in conjunction with the rest of the series.

Quilt series with activist intentions hold a particular power. Not only can the series tell that larger story, but it changes the physical scale of the project as a whole. A series of three or four or six quilts all speaking in concert takes on a different magnitude than an individual quilt. Here it is possible to overwhelm the viewer with the profusion of words, the expansiveness of the message. And ultimately that is the goal of quilts in series: to move beyond the scope of the singular quilt to produce something larger than the simple sum of its parts.

Funerary Quilts

THE CALLER TWICE SAID THAT
THE GUN WAS PROBABLY FAKE

Funerary Quilt #1: Tamir Rice, 60″ × 80″, 2020, designed and pieced by Thomas Knauer, quilted by Shelly Pagliai

Funerary Quilt #2: Stephon Clark, 60″ × 80″, 2021, designed and pieced by Thomas Knauer, quilted by Shelly Pagliai

E ONLY ITEM FOUND NEA
SUSPECT WAS A CELLPH

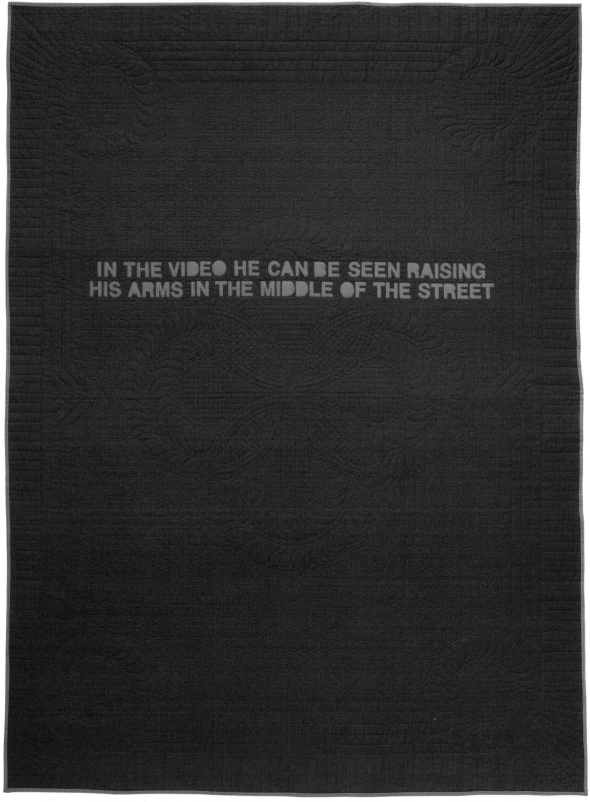

Funerary Quilt #3: Terence Crutcher, 60˝ × 80˝, 2021, designed and pieced by Thomas Knauer, quilted by Shelly Pagliai

Funerary Quilt #4: George Floyd, 60″ × 80″, 2022, designed and pieced by Thomas Knauer, quilted by Shelly Pagliai

NINE MINUTES AND TWENTY-NINE SECONDS

Funerary Quilt #5: Botham Jean, 60″ × 80″, 2022, designed and pieced by Thomas Knauer, quilted by Shelly Pagliai

These quilts use fragments of news stories to stand in for the whole of an event (a rhetorical device called synecdoche). Here each quilt highlights a tragic element of the police killing of an unarmed African American man (or boy, in the case of Tamir Rice) as a means to individualize events that we too often accept as inevitable. In using only a part of each story, the quilts allow viewers/readers space to call on their own knowledge, experience, and memories to flesh out the meaning and fill in the rest.

Here we see a parallel to how quilts themselves work. Quilts are so often stand-ins for the maker's presence for someone who lives at a distance, whether that be spatially or temporally. They mean more than their physical being, pointing to that larger meaning through their stitches and fabrics, labor, and love. In practice, all quilts are synecdochic objects.

Thus, the *Funerary Quilts* speak simultaneously of the individual events and of the epidemic of police killings of unarmed African Americans. The language on the quilts starts the viewer/reader with something very specific, which leads to larger things. My favorite text quilts are those that give a detail rather than try to present a whole story or an enormous idea all at once. Language blossoms with specifics and falls flat when reduced to generalities.

The Secret Life of Quilts

One of the amazing and powerful things about text is that it can ultimately point toward the lived world, the realm of people, places, and things. Language can point directly at something: The word *chair* can refer to a chair as a physical object. In this way language grows to encompass the whole of lived experience. A given text does not so much make a world as refer to one.

As such, a reference text on a quilt brings the referent—the thing—home, so to speak. In identifying an object with text on a quilt, I produce an association between the quilt and the referent of its text, spanning space and time to make that connection. Once the Amazon Specific Identification Number (ASIN) is used to find its correlating object, the quilt and that object are inextricably linked, and their meanings become entangled. The viewer/reader then combines the meaning associated with the particular object with the complex set of associations that quilts carry with them to create a larger set of ideas.

{B07SSK7

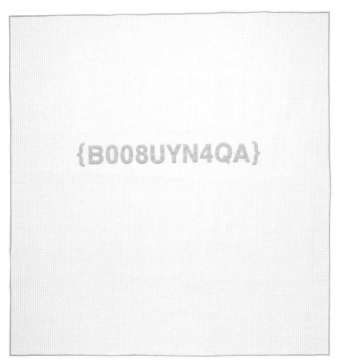

The Secret Life of Quilts (Amazon Specific Identification Code) #1, 80″ × 80″, 2022, designed and pieced by Thomas Knauer, quilted by Jennifer Strauser

The Secret Life of Quilts (Amazon Specific Identification Code) #2, 80″ × 80″, 2022, designed and pieced by Thomas Knauer, quilted by Jennifer Strauser

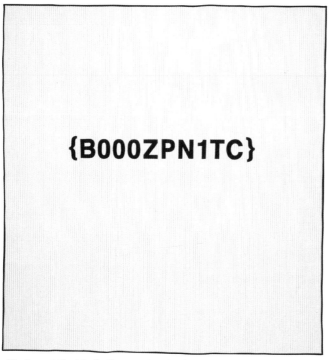

The Secret Life of Quilts (Amazon Specific Identification Code) #3, 80″ × 80″, 2022, designed and pieced by Thomas Knauer, quilted by Jennifer Strauser

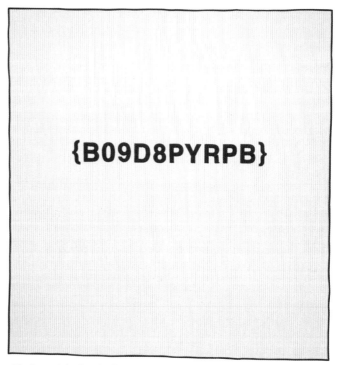

The Secret Life of Quilts (Amazon Specific Identification Code) #4, 80″ × 80″, 2022, designed and pieced by Thomas Knauer, quilted by Jennifer Strauser

My quilt series titled *The Secret Life of Quilts* uses just this idea. The letters and numbers may seem random and meaningless, but when they are brought together as a series, it becomes obvious that they definitely have a meaning, just one that is hidden. In this case, the sets of characters make up ASINs, and those ASINs refer to objects in a warehouse somewhere. The texts here simultaneously obscure the referenced objects even as those texts ultimately reveal them.

American Stories #1, #2, and #3

With this series I stripped away any semblance of metaphor or figurative language and plainly appliquéd each quilt with a different statistic about life in America. The statistics themselves are, or should be, horrifying, but they are so often easily glossed over in the seemingly endless cycle of terrible news. But having placed these texts on quilts, I like to imagine the quilts in use, being the first thing someone wakes up to and the last thing they see at night. Each of us can imagine what it would be like to sleep under, to live with, these quilts' terrible truths. That, in itself, is a powerful textual maneuver: to prevent words from becoming generalities and transform them into material reminders, especially of the things that should never be forgotten.

American Story #1: Poverty, 80″ × 80″, 2020, designed and pieced by Thomas Knauer, quilted by Jennifer Strauser

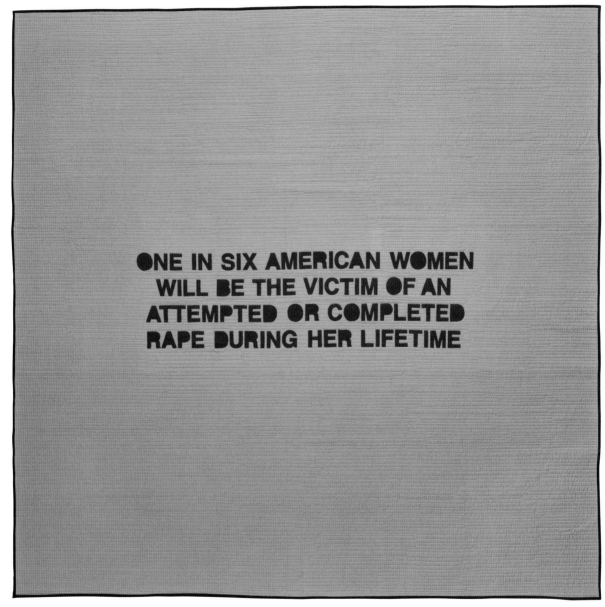

American Story #2: Rape, 80″ × 80″, 2020, designed and pieced by Thomas Knauer, quilted by Jennifer Strauser

American Story #3: Hunger, 80˝ × 80˝, 2020, designed and pieced by Thomas Knauer, quilted by Jennifer Strauser

AFTERWORD

WHILE not every quilt needs to be a text quilt, I think there is something unique about text quilts:

They ask viewers to encounter them on both an aesthetic and a linguistic level, engaging two parts of the brain to convey a message. As text is, for the time being, somewhat unexpected in the context of quilts, they catch viewers off guard and speak to them in surprising ways. And as language has so many possibilities, ranging from highly symbolic to literal, from encoded to direct, text quilts can convey a vast array of messages.

I make quilts as statements, as a means to address violence, inequity, and bigotry in its many forms. But every once in a while, I take a step back and use language playfully to speak in less directly critical ways. It is that range of possibility that keeps me making text quilts; I'm never quite sure what I am going to say until inspiration strikes. I find enjoyment in juggling the words, in playing with different arrangements and word choices, even when the quilt at hand is profoundly serious.

I think that is the nature of working with language in any form: It is something to be played with, mixed and remixed until the solution appears.

But on quilts, that text takes on an unexpected context, layering the meaning of the chosen language upon the historical meanings and attachments we associate with quilts. In this relation of text to quilt, one can work with contradiction or affirmation; the aesthetics of the quilt may support the statement or hold it in a stark contrast in which style and language simply do not mesh. The trick is to find the relationship that works for any given idea, to identify just where the complexity will reside: in the language itself or in the relationship of statement and style.

Of course there is a long history of text on quilts: signature quilts, temperance quilts, and more recently the monumental AIDS quilt. But I think we are at a moment of transition in quilting: More and more quilters are looking to say something with their craft, their art. Troubled times lead to extraordinary expression, and these are indeed troubled times. For me it is no wonder that I am seeing more and more text showing up on quilts: pieced and appliquéd, embroidered and printed. I think that we, as quilters, are finding our voices and are stepping forward to use them. This indeed may be a moment for quilting out loud.

ABOUT THE AUTHOR

Thomas Knauer lives in a small village in upstate New York with his wife, two children, a rabbit, and a dragon. He spends much of his time exploring the minutiae of letters and numbers, words and sentences. He loves words in just about any form, from letterpress printing to multimedia development. So it is no surprise that his work has taken a turn down the path of text-based quilts.

Photo by Katherine Terrell

He began his professional life teaching design at Drake University before turning to quilting. He has designed fabrics for several leading manufacturers, and his work has been exhibited in quilt shows and museums across the country, including the International Quilt Museum, the San Jose Museum of Quilts and Textiles, and the Quilt Festival in Houston.

His work typically focuses on issues of social justice and violence; his most recent body of work deals with the recent police shootings of unarmed African Americans. Knauer has authored several books in addition to *Quilt Out Loud* and plans to keep writing as long as people will let him. You can find him online at www.thomasknauersews.com.